THE SPIRITUAL EXERCISES

of ST. IGNATIUS *of* LOYOLA

ELDER MULLAN

Published by

GOLDEN BOOKMARK PUBLISHING

Email: goldenbookmarkpublishing@gmail.com

First published by GOLDEN BOOKMARK PUBLISHING in 2025

Golden Bookmark

Contents

I. Approbation Of The Latin Texts

The Exercises were offered for ecclesiastical censure at Rome. The text submitted was not, however, the one which is here reproduced, but two Latin translations, one in more polished Latin – since called the Vulgate Version – and one a literal rendering. The opinions expressed on these versions, as also the formal approval of Paul III, are given here, as applying quite entirely to the text from which the translations were made.

VULGATE VERSION

We have read everything compiled in the volume: it has greatly pleased us and seemed remarkably conducive to the salvation of souls. The Cardinal of Burgos

We grant leave to print the work; it is worthy of all praise and very profitable to the Christian profession. PHILIP, Vicar.

Such holy Exercises cannot but afford the greatest profit to any one who studies them. They should therefore be received with open arms. Fr. Aegidius Foscararius,

Master of the Sacred Palace

We have read these Spiritual Exercises, They greatly please us and we judge them worthy of being received and highly esteemed by all who practise the orthodox faith. The Cardinal of Burgos

We grant leave to print this work; it is worthy of all praise and very profitable to the Christian profession. PHILIP, Vicar.

As the Christian religion cannot long subsist without some spiritual exercises and meditations – for the Psalmist says: In my meditation a fire flames out – I think none more appropriate than these, which undoubtedly have had their source in the study of the Scriptures and in long experience. Fr. Aegidius Foscararius, Master of the Sacred Palace

PAUL III, POPE FOR A PERPETUAL REMEMBRANCE

The cares of the pastoral charge of the whole flock of Christ entrusted to Us and Our devotion to the glory and praise of God impel Us to embrace what helps the salvation of souls and their spiritual profit, and cause Us to hearken to those who petition Us for what can foster and nourish piety in the faithful.

So Our beloved son, Francis de Borgia, Duke of Gandia, has lately brought it to Our notice that Our beloved son Ignatius de Loyola, General of the Society of Jesus, erected by Us in Our beloved City and confirmed by Our Apostolic authority, has compiled certain instructions, or Spiritual Exercises, drawn from Holy Writ and from experience in the spiritual life, and has reduced them to an order which is excellently adapted to move piously the souls of the faithful, and that they are very useful and wholesome for the spiritual consolation and profit of the same. This the said Duke Francis has come to know by report from many places and by clear evidence at Barcelona, Valencia and Gandia.

Hence he has humbly begged Us to cause the aforesaid instructions and Spiritual Exercises to be examined, so that their fruit may be more spread, and more of the faithful may be induced to use them with greater devotion. And he has begged Us, should We find them worthy, to approve and praise them and out of Our Apostolic goodness to make other provision in the premisses.

We, therefore, have caused these instructions and Exercises to be examined, and by the testimony of and report made to Us by Our beloved son John Cardinal Priest of the Title of St. Clement, Bishop of Burgos and Inquisitor, Our venerable Brother Philip, Bishop of Saluciae, and Our Vicar General in things spiritual at Rome, and Our beloved son Aegidius Foscararius, Master of Our Sacred Palace, have found that these Exercises are full of piety and holiness and that they are and will be extremely useful and salutary for the spiritual profit of the faithful.

We have, besides, as We should, due regard to the rich fruits which Ignatius and the aforesaid Society founded by him are constantly producing everywhere in the Church of God, and to the very great help which the said Exercises have proved in this.

Moved, then, by this petition, with the aforesaid authority, by these presents, and of Our certain knowledge, We approve, praise, and favor with the present writing the aforesaid instructions and Exercises and all and everything contained in them, and We earnestly exhort all and each of the faithful of both sexes everywhere to employ instructions and Exercises so pious and to be instructed by them.

[Here follow regulations for the diffusion of the book, and then confirmatory clauses.]

Given at St. Mark's in Rome under the seal of the Fisherman, **31** July, **1548**, in the **14**th year of Our Pontificate. Blo. El. Fulginen.

II. Preface

THE present translation of the Exercises of St. Ignatius has been made from the Spanish Autograph of St. Ignatius. The copy so designated is not indeed in the handwriting of the Saint, but has a good number of corrections made by him and is known to have been used by him in giving the Exercises.

St. Ignatius of Loyola was a man without any great pretensions to education at the time he wrote this book. His native language was not Spanish, but Basque. His lack of education and his imperfect acquaintance with pure Spanish are enough to make it clear that a refined use of any language, and more especially of the Spanish, or, in general, anything like a finished or even perfectly correct, style is not to be expected in his work. Literary defects he removed to some extent, perhaps, as he continued to use and apply the book, but he is known never to have been fearful of such faults. His corrections found in this text are clearly made with a view to precision more than to anything else.

The Autograph of St. Ignatius was translated by Father General Roothaan into Latin and was reproduced by Father Rodeles in his edition of the Spanish text. But the original was not available to ordinary students. In **1908**, however, Father General Wernz allowed the entire book to be phototyped, and in this way it was spread throughout the Society of Jesus in a large number of copies. It is one of these which has been chiefly employed by the present translator, who has, besides, made frequent use of the Manuscript itself.

After considerable study of the matter, it seemed best to make this translation as faithful and close a reproduction of the Spanish text as could be. To do so it was necessary at times to sacrifice the niceties of style, but it was thought that those who would use the book would easily forego the elegancies of diction if they could feel sure they were reading the very words of St. Ignatius. Any other form of translation than the one adopted could hardly be kept from being a partial expansion, illustration or development of the original, and would therefore have proved, to some extent, a commentary as well as a translation. This the translator has earnestly sought to avoid, preferring to leave the further work of commentary to another occasion or to other hands.

Another reason for aiming at absolute fidelity rather than style was the fact that the Exercises are mostly read, not continuously for any time, but piecemeal and meditatively. Literary finish would therefore not be much sought or cared for in the book, but accuracy is. For this a certain neglect of style seemed pardonable in the translation, if only the real meaning of the writer could be made clear. Perhaps some may even find a charm in the consequent want of finish, seeing it reproduces more completely the style of St. Ignatius.

The process of translating in this way the Autograph text is not as simple as it might seem. The first difficulty is to make sure of the exact meaning of St. Ignatius. This is obscured, at times, by his language being that of nearly **400** years ago and being not pure Spanish. Occasionally, in fact, the Saint makes new Spanish words from the Latin or Italian, or uses Spanish words in an Italian or Latin sense, or employs phrases not current except in the Schools, and sometimes even has recourse to words in their Latin form. To be sure, then, of the meaning, one must often go to other languages and to the terms adopted in Scholastic Philosophy or Theology. The meaning clear, the further difficulty comes of finding an exactly equivalent English word or phrase.

In accomplishing his task, the translator has made free use of other translations, especially of that of Father General Roothaan into Latin, that of Father Venturi into Italian, and that of Father Jennesseaux into French, and has had the use of the literal translation into Latin made, apparently, by St. Ignatius himself, copied in **1541**, and formally approved by the Holy See in **1548**.

Besides the last-mentioned Manuscript and printed books, the translator has to acknowledge, as he does very gratefully, his obligations to the Very Rev. Father Mathias Abad, Father Achilles Gerste and particularly Father Mariano Lecina, Editor of the Ignatiana in the MONUMENTA HISTORICA S.J., for aid in appreciating the Spanish text, to Fathers Michael Ahern, Peter Cusick, Walter Drum, Francis Kemper and Herbert Noonan for general revision of the translation, and above all to Father Aloysius Frumveller for an accurate collation of the translation with the original.

In conclusion, it is well to warn the reader that the Spiritual Exercises of St. Ignatius are not meant to be read cursorily, but to be pondered word for word and under the direction of a competent guide. Read straight on, it may well appear jejune and unsatisfactory; studied in the actual making of the Exercises, the very text itself cannot fail to yield ever new material for thought and prayer.

ELDER MULLAN, S.J.
GERMAN COLLEGE, ROME,
Feast of St. Ignatius, **1909**.

III. General Note

In the reproduction of the text in English:

1. No change whatever is made in the wording. The proper corrections, however, of the two unimportant slips in quotation have been indicated in italics.

It may be remarked in passing that the text of Holy Scripture is not seldom given in the Spiritual Exercises in wording somewhat different from that of the Vulgate. Such divergences have not been noted in this translation. It will be remembered that, when the book was written, the Council of Trent had not yet put its seal on the Vulgate.

2. The head lines and the rubrics have been kept as they stand in the Manuscript. Where they were wanting, they have been supplied in italics.

3. Abbreviations have been filled out.

4. Wherever italics are used, the words in this character belong to the translator and not to St. Ignatius.

5. In the use of small and capital letters, and in the matter of punctuation and the division into paragraphs the practice of the copyist has usually not been followed. Various kinds of type, also, are used independently of the Manuscript.

6. As a matter of convenience, in citations from Holy Scripture, the modern method by chapter and verse is substituted for that of the Mss. chapter and letter. Besides, quotations are indicated by quotation marks in place of the parentheses of the Mss. Elder Mullan, S.J.

IV. Prayer Of Father Diertins

ROUSE up, O Lord, and foster the spirit of the Exercises which Blessed Ignatius labored to spread abroad, that we, too, may be filled with it and be zealous to love what he loved and do what he taught! Through Christ our Lord.
AMEN.

V. Annotations

To Give Some Understanding Of The Spiritual Exercises Which Follow, And To Enable Him Who Is To Give And Him Who Is To Receive Them To Help Themselves

First Annotation. The first Annotation is that by this name of Spiritual Exercises is meant every way of examining one's conscience, of meditating, of contemplating, of praying vocally and mentally, and of performing other spiritual actions, as will be said later. For as strolling, walking and running are bodily exercises, so every way of preparing and disposing the soul to rid itself of all the disordered tendencies, and, after it is rid, to seek and find the Divine Will as to the management of one's life for the salvation of the soul, is called a Spiritual Exercise.

Second Annotation.[1] The second is that the person who gives to another the way and order in which to meditate or contemplate, ought to relate faithfully the events of such Contemplation or Meditation, going over the Points with only a short or summary development. For, if the person who is making the Contemplation, takes the true groundwork of the narrative, and, discussing and considering for himself, finds something which makes the events a little clearer or brings them a little more home to him – whether this comes through his own reasoning, or because his intellect is enlightened by the Divine power – he will get more spiritual relish and fruit, than if he who is giving the Exercises had much explained and amplified the meaning of the events. For it is not knowing much, but realising and relishing things interiorly, that contents and satisfies the soul.

Third Annotation. The third: As in all the following Spiritual Exercises, we use acts of the intellect in reasoning, and acts of the will in movements of the feelings: let us remark that, in the acts of the will, when we are speaking vocally or mentally with God our Lord, or with His Saints, greater reverence is required on our part than when we are using the intellect in understanding.

Fourth Annotation. The fourth: The following Exercises are divided into four parts:

First, the consideration and contemplation on the sins;

Second, the life of Christ our Lord up to Palm Sunday inclusively;

Third, the Passion of Christ our Lord;

Fourth, the Resurrection and Ascension, with the three Methods of Prayer.

Though four weeks, to correspond to this division, are spent in the Exercises, it is not to be understood that each Week has, of necessity, seven or eight days. For, as it happens that in the First Week some are slower to find what they seek – namely, contrition, sorrow and tears for their sins – and in the same way some are more diligent than others, and more acted on or tried by different spirits; it is necessary sometimes to shorten the Week, and at other times to lengthen it. The same is true of all the other subsequent Weeks, seeking out the things according to the subject matter. However, the Exercises will be finished in thirty days, a little more or less.

Fifth Annotation. The fifth: It is very helpful to him who is receiving the Exercises to enter into them with great courage and generosity towards his Creator and Lord, offering[**2**] Him all his will and liberty, that His Divine Majesty may make use of his person and of all he has according[**3**] to His most Holy Will.

Sixth Annotation. The sixth: When he who is giving the Exercises sees that no spiritual movements, such as consolations or desolations, come to the soul of him who is exercising himself, and that he is not moved by different spirits, he ought to inquire carefully of him about the Exercises, whether he does them at their appointed times, and how. So too of the Additions, whether he observes them with diligence. Let him ask in detail about each of these things.

Consolation and desolation are spoken of on p. **170**; the Additions on p. **22**.

Seventh Annotation. The seventh: If he who is giving the Exercises sees that he who is receiving them is in desolation and tempted, let him not be hard or dissatisfied with him, but gentle and indulgent, giving him courage and strength for the future, and laying bare to him the wiles of the enemy of human nature, and getting him to prepare and dispose himself for the consolation coming.

Eighth Annotation. The eighth: If he who is giving the Exercises sees that he who is receiving them is in need of instruction about the desolations and wiles of the enemy – and the same of consolations – he may explain to him, as far as he needs them, the Rules of the First and Second Weeks for recognising different spirits. (P. **177**).

Ninth Annotation. The ninth is to notice, when he who is exercising himself is in the Exercises of the First Week, if he is a person who has not been versed in spiritual things, and is tempted grossly and openly – having, for example, suggested to him obstacles to going on in the service of God our Lord, such as labors, shame and fear for the honor of the world – let him who is giving the Exercises not explain to him the Rules of the Second Week for the discernment of spirits. Because, as much as those of the First Week will be helpful, those of the Second will be harmful to him, as being matter too subtle and too high for him to understand.

Tenth Annotation. The tenth: When he who is giving the Exercises perceives that he who is receiving them is assaulted and tempted under the appearance of good, then it is proper to instruct him about the Rules of the Second Week already mentioned. For, ordinarily, the enemy of human nature tempts under the appearance of good rather when the person is exercising himself in the Illuminative Life, which corresponds to the Exercises of the Second Week, and not so much in the Purgative Life, which corresponds to those of the First.

Eleventh Annotation. The eleventh: It is helpful to him who is receiving the Exercises in the First Week, not to know anything of what he is to do in the Second, but so to labor in the First to attain the object he is seeking as if he did not hope to find in the Second any good.

Twelfth Annotation. The twelfth: As he who is receiving the Exercises is to give an hour to each of the five Exercises or Contemplations which will be made every day, he who is giving the Exercises has to warn him carefully to always see that his soul remains content in the consciousness of having been a full hour in the Exercise, and rather more than less. For the enemy is not a little used to try and make one cut short the hour of such contemplation, meditation or prayer.

Thirteenth Annotation. The thirteenth: It is likewise to be remarked that, as, in the time of consolation, it is easy and not irksome to be in contemplation the full hour, so it is very hard in the time of desolation to fill it out. For this reason, the person who is exercising himself, in order to act against the desolation and conquer the temptations, ought always to stay somewhat more than the full hour; so as to accustom himself not only to resist the adversary, but even to overthrow him.

Fourteenth Annotation. The fourteenth: If he who is giving the Exercises sees that he who is receiving them is going on in consolation and with much fervor, he ought to warn him not to make any inconsiderate and hasty promise or vow: and the more light of character he knows him to be, the more he ought to warn and admonish him. For, though one may justly influence another to embrace the religious life, in which he is understood to make vows of obedience, poverty and chastity, and, although a good work done under vow is more meritorious than one done without it, one should carefully consider the circumstances and personal qualities of the individual and how much help or hindrance he is likely to find in fulfilling the thing he would want to promise.

Fifteenth Annotation. The fifteenth: He who is giving the Exercises ought not to influence him who is receiving them more to poverty or to a promise, than to their opposites, nor more to one state or way of life than to another. For though, outside the Exercises, we can lawfully and with merit influence every one who is probably fit to choose continence, virginity, the religious life and all manner of evangelical perfection, still in the Spiritual Exercises, when seeking the Divine Will, it is more fitting and much better, that the Creator and Lord Himself should communicate Himself to His devout soul, inflaming it with His love and praise, and disposing it for the way in which it will be better able to serve Him in future. So, he who is giving the Exercises should not turn or incline to one side or the other, but standing in the centre like a balance, leave the Creator to act immediately with the creature, and the creature with its Creator and Lord.

Sixteenth Annotation. The sixteenth: For this – namely, that the Creator and Lord may work more surely in His creature – it is very expedient, if it happens that the soul is attached or inclined to a thing inordinately, that one should move himself, putting forth all his strength, to come to the contrary of what he is wrongly drawn to. Thus if he inclines to seeking and possessing an office or benefice, not for the honor and glory of God our Lord, nor for the spiritual well-being of souls, but for his own temporal advantage and interests, he ought to excite his feelings to the contrary, being instant in prayers and other spiritual exercises, and asking God our Lord for the contrary, namely, not to want such office or benefice, or any other thing, unless His Divine Majesty, putting his desires in order, change his first inclination for him, so that the motive for desiring or having one thing or another be only the service, honor, and glory of His Divine Majesty.

Seventeenth Annotation. The seventeenth: It is very helpful that he who is giving the Exercises, without wanting to ask or know from him who is receiving them his personal thoughts or sins, should be faithfully informed of the various movements and thoughts which the different spirits put in him. For, according as is more or less useful for him, he can give him some spiritual Exercises suited and adapted to the need of such a soul so acted upon.

Eighteenth Annotation. The eighteenth: The Spiritual Exercises have to be adapted to the dispositions of the persons who wish to receive them, that is, to their age, education or ability, in order not to give to one who is uneducated or of little intelligence things he cannot easily bear and profit by.

Again, that should be given to each one by which, according to his wish to dispose himself, he may be better able to help himself and to profit.

So, to him who wants help to be instructed and to come to a certain degree of contentment of soul, can be given the Particular Examen, p. **21**, and then the General Examen, p. **25**; also, for a half hour in the morning, the Method of Prayer on the Commandments, the Deadly Sins, etc., p. **125**. Let him be recommended, also, to confess his sins every eight days, and, if he can, to receive the Blessed Sacrament every fifteen days, and better, if he be so moved, every eight. This way is more proper for illiterate or less educated persons. Let each of the Commandments be explained to them; and so of the Deadly Sins, Precepts of the Church, Five Senses, and Works of Mercy.

So, too, should he who is giving the Exercises observe that he who is receiving them has little ability or little natural capacity, from whom not much fruit is to be hoped, it is more expedient to give him some of these easy Exercises, until he confesses his sins. Then let him be given some Examens of Conscience and some method for going to Confession oftener than was his custom, in order to preserve what he has gained, but let him not go on into the matter of the Election, or into any other Exercises that are outside the First Week, especially when more progress can be made in other persons and there is not time for every thing.

Nineteenth Annotation. The nineteenth: A person of education or ability who is taken up with public affairs or suitable business, may take an hour and a half daily to exercise himself.

Let the end for which man is created be explained to him, and he can also be given for the space of a half-hour the Particular Examen and then the General and the way to confess and to receive the Blessed Sacrament. Let him, during three days every morning, for the space of an hour, make the meditation on the First, Second and Third Sins, pp. **37**, **38**; then, three other days at the same hour, the meditation on the statement of Sins, p. **40**; then, for three other days at the same hour, on the punishments corresponding to Sins, p. **45**. Let him be given in all three meditations the ten Additions, p. **47**.

For the mysteries of Christ our Lord, let the same course be kept, as is explained below and in full in the Exercises themselves.

Twentieth Annotation. The twentieth: To him who is more disengaged, and who desires to get all the profit he can, let all the Spiritual Exercises be given in the order in which they follow.

In these he will, ordinarily, more benefit himself, the more he separates himself from all friends and acquaintances and from all earthly care, as by changing from the house where he was dwelling, and taking another house or room to live in, in as much privacy as he can, so that it be in his power to go each day to Mass and to Vespers, without fear that his acquaintances will put obstacles in his way.

From this isolation three chief benefits, among many others, follow.

The first is that a man, by separating himself from many friends and acquaintances, and likewise from many not well-ordered affairs, to serve and praise God our Lord, merits no little in the sight of His Divine Majesty.

The second is, that being thus isolated, and not having his understanding divided on many things, but concentrating his care on one only, namely, on serving his Creator and benefiting his own soul, he uses with greater freedom his natural powers, in seeking with diligence what he so much desires.

The third: the more our soul finds itself alone and isolated, the more apt it makes itself to approach and to reach its Creator and Lord, and the more it so approaches Him, the more it disposes itself to receive graces and gifts from His Divine and Sovereign Goodness.

VI. Presupposition

Spiritual Exercises To Conquer Oneself And Regulate One's Life Without Determining Oneself Through [4] Any Tendency That Is Disordered

In order that both he who is giving the Spiritual Exercises, and he who is receiving them, may more help and benefit themselves, let it be presupposed that every good Christian is to be more ready to save his neighbor's proposition than to condemn it. If he cannot save it, let him inquire how he means it; and if he means it badly, let him correct him with charity. If that is not enough, let him seek all the suitable means to bring him to mean it well, and save himself.

VII. First Week

Principle And Foundation

Man is created to praise, reverence, and serve God our Lord, and by this means to save his soul.

And the other things on the face of the earth are created for man and that they may help him in prosecuting the end for which he is created.

From this it follows that man is to use them as much as they help him on to his end, and ought to rid himself of them so far as they hinder him as to it.

For this it is necessary to make ourselves indifferent to all created things in all that is allowed to the choice of our free will and is not prohibited to it; so that, on our part, we want not health rather than sickness, riches rather than poverty, honor rather than dishonor, long rather than short life, and so in all the rest; desiring and choosing only what is most conducive for us to the end for which we are created.

PARTICULAR AND DAILY EXAMEN

It contains in it three times, and two to examine oneself.

The first time is in the morning, immediately on rising, when one ought to propose to guard himself with diligence against that particular sin or defect which he wants to correct and amend.

The second time is after dinner, when one is to ask of God our Lord what one wants, namely, grace to remember how many times he has fallen into that particular sin or defect, and to amend himself in the future. Then let him make the first Examen, asking account of his soul of that particular thing proposed, which he wants to correct and amend. Let him go over hour by hour, or period by period, commencing at the hour he rose, and continuing up to the hour and instant of the present examen, and let him make in the first line of the G—— as many dots as were the times he has fallen into that particular sin or defect. Then let him resolve anew to amend himself up to the second Examen which he will make.

The third time: After supper, the second Examen will be made, in the same way, hour by hour, commencing at the first Examen and continuing up to the present (second) one, and let him make in the second line of the same G—— as many dots as were the times he has fallen into that particular sin or defect.

FOUR ADDITIONS FOLLOW TO RID ONESELF SOONER OF THAT PARTICULAR SIN OR DEFECT

First Addition. The first Addition is that each time one falls into that particular sin or defect, let him put his hand on his breast, grieving for having fallen: which can be done even in the presence of many, without their perceiving what he is doing.

Second Addition. The second: As the first line of the G—— means the first Examen, and the second line the second Examen, let him look at night if there is amendment from the first line to the second, that is, from the first Examen to the second.

Third Addition. The third: To compare the second day with the first; that is, the two Examens of the present day with the other two Examens of the previous day, and see if he has amended himself from one day to the other.

Fourth Addition. The fourth Addition: To compare one week with another, and see if he has amended himself in the present week over the week past.

Note. It is to be noted that the first (large) G—— which follows means the

Sunday: the second (smaller), the Monday: the third, the Tuesday, and so on.

GENERAL EXAMEN OF CONSCIENCE TO PURIFY ONESELF AND TO MAKE ONE'S CONFESSION BETTER

I presuppose that there are three kinds of thoughts in me: that is, one my own, which springs from my mere liberty and will; and two others, which come from without, one from the good spirit, and the other from the bad.

THOUGHT

There are two ways of meriting in the bad thought which comes from without, namely:

First Way. A thought of committing a mortal sin, which thought I resist immediately and it remains conquered.

Second Way. The second way of meriting is: When that same bad thought comes to me and I resist it, and it returns to me again and again, and I always resist, until it is conquered.

This second way is more meritorious than the first.

A venial sin is committed when the same thought comes of sinning mortally and one gives ear to it, making some little delay, or receiving some sensual pleasure, or when there is some negligence in rejecting such thought.

There are two ways of sinning mortally:

First Way. The first is, when one gives consent to the bad thought, to act afterwards as he has consented, or to put it in act if he could.

Second Way. The second way of sinning mortally is when that sin is put in act.

This is a greater sin for three reasons: first, because of the greater time; second, because of the greater intensity; third, because of the greater harm to the two persons.

WORD

One must not swear, either by Creator or creature, if it be not with truth, necessity and reverence.

By necessity I mean, not when any truth whatever is affirmed with oath, but when it is of some importance for the good of the soul, or the body, or for temporal goods.

By reverence I mean when, in naming the Creator and Lord, one acts with consideration, so as to render Him the honor and reverence due.

It is to be noted that, though in an idle oath one sins more when he swears by the Creator than by the creature, it is more difficult to swear in the right way with truth, necessity and reverence by the creature than by the Creator, for the following reasons.

First Reason. The first: When we want to swear by some creature, wanting to name the creature does not make us so attentive or circumspect as to telling the truth, or as to affirming it with necessity, as would wanting to name the Lord and Creator of all things.

Second Reason. The second is that in swearing by the creature it is not so easy to show reverence and respect to the Creator, as in swearing and naming the same Creator and Lord, because wanting to name God our Lord brings with it more respect and reverence than wanting to name the created thing. Therefore swearing by the creature is more allowable to the perfect than to the imperfect, because the perfect, through continued contemplation and enlightenment of intellect, consider, meditate and contemplate more that God our Lord is in every creature, according to His own essence, presence and power, and so in swearing by the creature they are more apt and prepared than the imperfect to show respect and reverence to their Creator and Lord.

Third Reason. The third is that in continually swearing by the creature, idolatry is to be more feared in the imperfect than in the perfect.

One must not speak an idle word. By idle word I mean one which does not benefit either me or another, and is not directed to that intention. Hence words spoken for any useful purpose, or meant to profit one's own or another's soul, the body or temporal goods, are never idle, not even if one were to speak of something foreign to one's state of life, as, for instance, if a religious speaks of wars or articles of trade; but in all that is said there is merit in directing well, and sin in directing badly, or in speaking idly.

Nothing must be said to injure another's character or to find fault, because if I reveal a mortal sin that is not public, I sin mortally; if a venial sin, venially; and if a defect, I show a defect of my own.

But if the intention is right, in two ways one can speak of the sin or fault of another:

First Way. The first: When the sin is public, as in the case of a public prostitute, and of a sentence given in judgment, or of a public error which is infecting the souls with whom one comes in contact.

Second Way. Second: When the hidden sin is revealed to some person that he may help to raise him who is in sin – supposing, however, that he has some probable conjectures or grounds for thinking that he will be able to help him.

ACT

Taking the Ten Commandments, the Precepts of the Church and the recommendations of Superiors, every act done against any of these three heads is, according to its greater or less nature, a greater or a lesser sin.

By recommendations of Superiors I mean such things as Bulls de Cruzadas and other Indulgences, as for instance for peace, granted under condition of going to Confession and receiving the Blessed Sacrament. For one commits no little sin in being the cause of others acting contrary to such pious exhortations and recommendations of our Superiors, or in doing so oneself.

METHOD FOR MAKING THE GENERAL EXAMEN

It contains in it five Points.

First Point. The first Point is to give thanks to God our Lord for the benefits received.

Second Point. The second, to ask grace to know our sins and cast them out.

Third Point. The third, to ask account of our soul from the hour that we rose up to the present Examen, hour by hour, or period by period: and first as to thoughts, and then as to words, and then as to acts, in the same order as was mentioned in the Particular Examen.

Fourth Point. The fourth, to ask pardon of God our Lord for the faults.

Fifth Point. The fifth, to purpose amendment with His grace.

OUR FATHER.

GENERAL CONFESSION WITH COMMUNION

Whoever, of his own accord, wants to make a General Confession, will, among many other advantages, find three in making it here.

First. The first: Though whoever goes to Confession every year is not obliged to make a General Confession, by making it there is greater profit and merit, because of the greater actual sorrow for all the sins and wickedness of his whole life.

Second. The second: In the Spiritual Exercises, sins and their malice are understood more intimately, than in the time when one was not so giving himself to interior things. Gaining now more knowledge of and sorrow for them, he will have greater profit and merit than he had before.

Third. The third is: In consequence, having made a better Confession and being better disposed, one finds himself in condition and prepared to receive the Blessed Sacrament: the reception of which is an aid not only not to fall into sin, but also to preserve the increase of grace.

This General Confession will be best made immediately after the Exercises of the First Week.

FIRST EXERCISE

IT IS A MEDITATION WITH THE THREE POWERS ON THE FIRST, THE SECOND AND THE THIRD SIN

It contains in it, after one Preparatory Prayer and two Preludes, three chief Points and one Colloquy.

Prayer. The Preparatory Prayer is to ask grace of God our Lord that all my intentions, actions and operations may be directed purely to the service and praise of His Divine Majesty.

First Prelude. The First Prelude is a composition, seeing the place.

Here it is to be noted that, in a visible contemplation or meditation – as, for instance, when one contemplates Christ our Lord, Who is visible – the composition will be to see with the sight of the imagination the corporeal place where the thing is found which I want to contemplate. I say the corporeal place, as for instance, a Temple or Mountain where Jesus Christ or Our Lady is found, according to what I want to contemplate. In an invisible contemplation or meditation – as here on the Sins – the composition will be to see with the sight of the imagination and consider that my soul is imprisoned in this corruptible body, and all the compound in this valley, as exiled among brute beasts: I say all the compound of soul and body.

Second Prelude. The second is to ask God our Lord for what I want and desire.

The petition has to be according to the subject matter; that is, if the contemplation is on the Resurrection, one is to ask for joy with Christ in joy; if it is on the Passion, he is to ask for pain, tears and torment with Christ in torment.

Here it will be to ask shame and confusion at myself, seeing how many have been damned for only one mortal sin, and how many times I deserved to be condemned forever for my so many sins.

Note. Before all Contemplations or Meditations, there ought always to be made the Preparatory Prayer, which is not changed, and the two Preludes already mentioned, which are sometimes changed, according to the subject matter.

First Point. The first Point will be to bring the memory on the First Sin, which was that of the Angels, and then to bring the intellect on the same, discussing it; then the will, wanting to recall and understand all this in order to make me more ashamed and confound me more, bringing into comparison with the one sin of the Angels my so many sins, and reflecting, while they for one sin were cast into Hell, how often I have deserved it for so many.

I say to bring to memory the sin of the Angels, how they, being created in grace, not wanting to help themselves with their liberty to reverence and obey their Creator and Lord, coming to pride, were changed from grace to malice, and hurled from Heaven to Hell; and so then to discuss more in detail with the intellect: and then to move the feelings more with the will.

Second Point. The second is to do the same – that is, to bring the Three Powers – on the sin of Adam and Eve, bringing to memory how on account of that sin they did penance for so long a time, and how much corruption came on the human race, so many people going the way to Hell.

I say to bring to memory the Second Sin, that of our First Parents; how after Adam was created in the field of Damascus and placed in the Terrestrial Paradise, and Eve was created from his rib, being forbidden to eat of the Tree of Knowledge, they ate and so sinned, and afterwards clothed in tunics of skins and cast from Paradise, they lived, all their life, without the original justice which they had lost, and in many labors and much penance. And then to discuss with the understanding more in detail; and to use the will as has been said.

Third Point. The third is likewise to do the same on the Third particular Sin of any one who for one mortal sin is gone to Hell – and many others without number, for fewer sins than I have committed.

I say to do the same on the Third particular Sin, bringing to memory the gravity and malice of the sin against one's Creator and Lord; to discuss with the understanding how in sinning and acting against the Infinite Goodness, he has been justly condemned forever; and to finish with the will as has been said.

Colloquy. Imagining Christ our Lord present and placed on the Cross, let me make a Colloquy, how from Creator He is come to making Himself man, and from life eternal is come to temporal death, and so to die for my sins.

Likewise, looking at myself, what I have done for Christ, what I am doing for Christ, what I ought to do for Christ.

And so, seeing Him such, and so nailed on the Cross, to go over that which will present itself.

The Colloquy is made, properly speaking, as one friend speaks to another, or as a servant to his master; now asking some grace, now blaming oneself for some misdeed, now communicating one's affairs, and asking advice in them.

And let me say an OUR FATHER.

SECOND EXERCISE

IT IS A MEDITATION ON THE SINS AND CONTAINS IN IT AFTER THE PREPARATORY PRAYER AND TWO PRELUDES, FIVE POINTS AND ONE COLLOQUY

Prayer. Let the Preparatory Prayer be the same.

First Prelude. The First Prelude will be the same composition.

Second Prelude. The second is to ask for what I want. It will be here to beg a great and intense sorrow and tears for my sins.

First Point. The first Point is the statement of the sins; that is to say, to bring to memory all the sins of life, looking from year to year, or from period to period. For this three things are helpful: first, to look at the place and the house where I have lived; second, the relations I have had with others; third, the occupation in which I have lived.

Second Point. The second, to weigh the sins, looking at the foulness and the malice which any mortal sin committed has in it, even supposing it were not forbidden.

Third Point. The third, to look at who I am, lessening myself by examples:

First, how much I am in comparison to all men;

Second, what men are in comparison to all the Angels and Saints of Paradise;

Third, what all Creation is in comparison to God: (–Then I alone, what can I be?)

Fourth, to see all my bodily corruption and foulness;

Fifth, to look at myself as a sore and ulcer, from which have sprung so many sins and so many iniquities and so very vile poison.

Fourth Point. The fourth, to consider what God is, against Whom I have sinned, according to His attributes; comparing them with their contraries in me – His Wisdom with my ignorance; His Omnipotence with my weakness; His Justice with my iniquity; His Goodness with my malice.

Fifth Point. The fifth, an exclamation of wonder with deep feeling, going through all creatures, how they have left me in life and preserved me in it; the Angels, how, though they are the sword of the Divine Justice, they have endured me, and guarded me, and prayed for me; the Saints, how they have been engaged in interceding and praying for me; and the heavens, sun, moon, stars, and elements, fruits, birds, fishes and animals – and the earth, how it has not opened to swallow me up, creating new Hells for me to suffer in them forever!

Colloquy. Let me finish with a Colloquy of mercy, pondering and giving thanks to God our Lord that He has given me life up to now, proposing amendment, with His grace, for the future.

OUR FATHER.

THIRD EXERCISE

IT IS A REPETITION OF THE FIRST AND SECOND EXERCISE, MAKING THREE COLLOQUIES

After the Preparatory Prayer and two Preludes, it will be to repeat the First and Second Exercise, marking and dwelling on the Points in which I have felt greater consolation or desolation, or greater spiritual feeling.

After this I will make three Colloquies in the following manner:

First Colloquy. The first Colloquy to Our Lady, that she may get me grace from Her Son and Lord for three things: first, that I may feel an interior knowledge of my sins, and hatred of them; second, that I may feel the disorder of my actions, so that, hating them, I may correct myself and put myself in order; third, to ask knowledge of the world, in order that, hating it, I may put away from me worldly and vain things.

And with that a HAIL MARY.

Second Colloquy. The second: The same to the Son, begging Him to get it for me from the Father.

And with that the SOUL OF CHRIST.

Third Colloquy. The third: The same to the Father, that the Eternal Lord Himself may grant it to me.

And with that an OUR FATHER.

FOURTH EXERCISE

IT IS A SUMMARY OF THIS SAME THIRD

I said a summary, that the understanding, without wandering, may assiduously go through the memory of the things contemplated in the preceding Exercises.

I will make the same three Colloquies.

FIFTH EXERCISE

IT IS A MEDITATION ON HELL

It contains in it, after the Preparatory Prayer and two Preludes, five Points and one Colloquy:

Prayer. Let the Preparatory Prayer be the usual one.

First Prelude. The first Prelude is the composition, which is here to see with the sight of the imagination the length, breadth and depth of Hell.

Second Prelude. The second, to ask for what I want: it will be here to ask for interior sense of the pain which the damned suffer, in order that, if, through my faults, I should forget the love of the Eternal Lord, at least the fear of the pains may help me not to come into sin.

First Point. The first Point will be to see with the sight of the imagination the great fires, and the souls as in bodies of fire.

Second Point. The second, to hear with the ears wailings, howlings, cries, blasphemies against Christ our Lord and against all His Saints.

Third Point. The third, to smell with the smell smoke, sulphur, dregs and putrid things.

Fourth Point. The fourth, to taste with the taste bitter things, like tears, sadness and the worm of conscience.

Fifth Point. The fifth, to touch with the touch; that is to say, how the fires touch and burn the souls.

Colloquy. Making a Colloquy to Christ our Lord, I will bring to memory the souls that are in Hell, some because they did not believe the Coming, others because, believing, they did not act according to His Commandments; making three divisions:

First, Second, and Third Divisions. The first, before the Coming; the second, during His life; the third, after His life in this world; and with this I will give Him thanks that He has not let me fall into any of these divisions, ending my life.

Likewise, I will consider how up to now He has always had so great pity and mercy on me.

I will end with an OUR FATHER.

Note. The first Exercise will be made at midnight; the second immediately on rising in the morning; the third, before or after Mass; in any case, before dinner; the fourth at the hour of Vespers; the fifth, an hour before supper.

This arrangement of hours, more or less, I always mean in all the four Weeks, according as his age, disposition and physical condition help the person who is exercising himself to make five Exercises or fewer.

ADDITIONS

TO MAKE THE EXERCISES BETTER AND TO FIND BETTER WHAT ONE DESIRES

First Addition. The first Addition is, after going to bed, just when I want to go asleep, to think, for the space of a HAIL MARY, of the hour that I have to rise and for what, making a resume of the Exercise which I have to make.

Second Addition. The second: When I wake up, not giving place to any other thought, to turn my attention immediately to what I am going to contemplate in the first Exercise, at midnight, bringing myself to confusion for my so many sins, setting examples, as, for instance, if a knight found himself before his king and all his court, ashamed and confused at having much offended him, from whom he had first received many gifts and many favors: in the same way, in the second Exercise, making myself a great sinner and in chains; that is to say going to appear bound as in chains before the Supreme Eternal Judge; taking for an example how prisoners in chains and already deserving death, appear before their temporal judge. And I will dress with these thoughts or with others, according to the subject matter.

Third Addition. The third: A step or two before the place where I have to contemplate or meditate, I will put myself standing for the space of an OUR FATHER, my intellect raised on high, considering how God our Lord is looking at me, etc.; and will make an act of reverence or humility.

Fourth Addition. The fourth: To enter on the contemplation now on my knees, now prostrate on the earth, now lying face upwards, now seated, now standing, always intent on seeking what I want.

We will attend to two things. The first is, that if I find what I want kneeling, I will not pass on; and if prostrate, likewise, etc. The second; in the Point in which I find what I want, there I will rest, without being anxious to pass on, until I content myself.

Fifth Addition. The fifth: After finishing the Exercise, I will, during the space of a quarter of an hour, seated or walking leisurely, look how it went with me in the Contemplation or Meditation; and if badly, I will look for the cause from which it proceeds, and having so seen it, will be sorry, in order to correct myself in future; and if well, I will give thanks to God our Lord, and will do in like manner another time.

Sixth Addition. The sixth: Not to want to think on things of pleasure or joy, such as heavenly glory, the Resurrection, etc. Because whatever consideration of joy and gladness hinders our feeling pain and grief and shedding tears for our sins: but to keep before me that I want to grieve and feel pain, bringing to memory rather Death and Judgment.

Seventh Addition. The seventh: For the same end, to deprive myself of all light, closing the blinds and doors while I am in the room, if it be not to recite prayers, to read and eat.

Eighth Addition. The eighth: Not to laugh nor say a thing provocative of laughter.

Ninth Addition. The ninth: To restrain my sight, except in receiving or dismissing the person with whom I have spoken.

Tenth Addition. The tenth Addition is penance.

This is divided into interior and exterior. The interior is to grieve for one's sins, with a firm purpose of not committing them nor any others. The exterior, or fruit of the first, is chastisement for the sins committed, and is chiefly taken in three ways.

First Way. The first is as to eating. That is to say, when we leave off the superfluous, it is not penance, but temperance. It is penance when we leave off from the suitable; and the more and more, the greater and better – provided that the person does not injure himself, and that no notable illness follows.

Second Way. The second, as to the manner of sleeping. Here too it is not penance to leave off the superfluous of delicate or soft things, but it is penance when one leaves off from the suitable in the manner: and the more and more, the better – provided that the person does not injure himself and no notable illness follows. Besides, let not anything of the suitable sleep be left off, unless in order to come to the mean, if one has a bad habit of sleeping too much.

Third Way. The third, to chastise the flesh, that is, giving it sensible pain, which is given by wearing haircloth or cords or iron chains next to the flesh, by scourging or wounding oneself, and by other kinds of austerity.

Note. What appears most suitable and most secure with regard to penance is that the pain should be sensible in the flesh and not enter within the bones, so that it give pain and not illness. For this it appears to be more suitable to scourge oneself with thin cords, which give pain exteriorly, rather than in another way which would cause notable illness within.

First Note. The first Note is that the exterior penances are done chiefly for three ends: First, as satisfaction for the sins committed;

Second, to conquer oneself – that is, to make sensuality obey reason and all inferior parts be more subject to the superior;

Third, to seek and find some grace or gift which the person wants and desires; as, for instance, if he desires to have interior contrition for his sins, or to weep much over them, or over the pains and sufferings which Christ our Lord suffered in His Passion, or to settle some doubt in which the person finds himself.

Second Note. The second: It is to be noted that the first and second Addition have to be made for the Exercises of midnight and at daybreak, but not for those which will be made at other times; and the fourth Addition will never be made in church in the presence of others, but in private, as at home, etc.

Third Note. The third: When the person who is exercising himself does not yet find what he desires – as tears, consolations, etc., – it often helps for him to make a change in food, in sleep and in other ways of doing penance, so that he change himself, doing penance two or three days, and two or three others not. For it suits some to do more penance and others less, and we often omit doing penance from sensual love and from an erroneous judgment that the human system will not be able to bear it without notable illness; and sometimes, on the contrary, we do too much, thinking that the body can bear it; and as God our Lord knows our nature infinitely better, often in such changes He gives each one to perceive what is suitable for him.

Fourth Note. The fourth: Let the Particular Examen be made to rid oneself of defects and negligences on the Exercises and Additions. And so in the SECOND, THIRD AND FOURTH WEEKS.

VIII. Second Week

THE CALL OF THE TEMPORAL KING

IT HELPS TO CONTEMPLATE THE LIFE OF THE KING ETERNAL

Prayer. Let the Preparatory Prayer be the usual one.

First Prelude. The first Prelude is a composition, seeing the place: it will be here to see with the sight of the imagination, the synagogues,[**5**] villages and towns through which Christ our Lord preached.

Second Prelude. The second, to ask for the grace which I want: it will be here to ask grace of our Lord that I may not be deaf to His call, but ready and diligent to fulfill His most Holy Will.

First Point. The first Point is, to put before me a human king chosen by God our Lord, whom all Christian princes and men reverence and obey.

Second Point. The second, to look how this king speaks to all his people, saying: "It is my Will to conquer all the land of unbelievers. Therefore, whoever would like to come with me is to be content to eat as I, and also to drink and dress, etc., as I: likewise he is to labor like me [**6**] in the day and watch in the night, etc., that so afterwards he may have part with me in the victory, as he has had it in the labors."

Third Point. The third, to consider what the good subjects ought to answer to a King so liberal and so kind, and hence, if any one did not accept the appeal of such a king, how deserving he would be of being censured by all the world, and held for a mean-spirited knight.

IN PART 2

The second part of this Exercise consists in applying the above parable of the temporal King to Christ our Lord, conformably to the three Points mentioned.

First Point. And as to the first Point, if we consider such a call of the temporal King to his subjects, how much more worthy of consideration is it to see Christ our Lord, King eternal, and before Him all the entire world, which and each one in particular He calls, and says: "It is My will to conquer all the world and all enemies and so to enter into the glory of My Father; therefore, whoever would like to come with Me is to labor with Me, that following Me in the pain, he may also follow Me in the glory."

Second Point. The second, to consider that all those who have judgment and reason will offer their entire selves to the labor.

Third Point. The third, those who will want to be more devoted and signalise themselves in all service of their King Eternal and universal Lord, not only will offer their persons to the labor, but even, acting against their own sensuality and against their carnal and worldly love, will make offerings of greater value and greater importance, saying:

"Eternal Lord of all things, I make my oblation with Thy favor and help, in presence of Thy infinite Goodness and in presence of Thy glorious Mother and of all the Saints of the heavenly Court; that I want and desire, and it is my deliberate determination, if only it be Thy greater service and praise, to imitate Thee in bearing all injuries and all abuse and all poverty of spirit, and actual poverty, too, if Thy most Holy Majesty wants to choose and receive me to such life and state."

First Note. This Exercise will be made twice in the day; namely, in the morning on rising and an hour before dinner or before supper.

Second Note. For the Second Week and so on, it is very helpful to read at intervals in the books of the Imitation of Christ, or of the Gospels, and of lives of Saints.

THE FIRST DAY AND FIRST CONTEMPLATION

It is on the incarnation and contains the preparatory prayer, three preludes, three points and one colloquy

Prayer. The usual Preparatory Prayer.

First Prelude. The first Prelude is to bring up the narrative of the thing which I have to contemplate.

Here, it is how the Three Divine Persons looked at all the plain or circuit of all the world, full of men, and how, seeing that all were going down to Hell, it is determined in Their Eternity,[**7**] that the Second Person shall become man to save the human race, and so, the fullness of times being come,[**8**] They sent the Angel St. Gabriel to Our Lady (p. **133**).

Second Prelude. The second, a composition, seeing the place: here it will be to see the great capacity and circuit of the world, in which are so many and such different people: then likewise, in particular, the house and rooms of Our Lady in the city of Nazareth, in the Province of Galilee.

Third Prelude. The third, to ask for what I want: it will be to ask for interior knowledge of the Lord, Who for me has become man, that I may more love and follow Him.

Note. It is well to note here that this same Preparatory Prayer, without changing it, as was said in the beginning, and the same three Preludes, are to be made in this Week and in the others following, changing the form according to the subject matter.

First Point. The first Point is, to see the various persons: and first those on the surface of the earth, in such variety, in dress as in actions: some white and others black; some in peace and others in war; some weeping and others laughing; some well, others ill; some being born and others dying, etc.

2. To see and consider the Three Divine Persons, as on their royal throne or seat of Their Divine Majesty, how They look on all the surface and circuit of the earth, and all the people in such blindness, and how they are dying and going down to Hell.

3. To see Our Lady, and the Angel who is saluting her, and to reflect in order to get profit from such a sight.

Second Point. The second, to hear what the persons on the face of the earth are saying, that is, how they are talking with one another, how they swear and blaspheme, etc.; and likewise what the Divine Persons are saying, that is: "Let Us work the redemption of the Human race," etc.; and then what the Angel and Our Lady are saying; and to reflect then so as to draw profit from their words.

Third Point. The third, to look then at what the persons on the face of the earth are doing, as, for instance, killing, going to Hell etc.; likewise what the Divine Persons are doing, namely, working out the most holy Incarnation, etc.; and likewise what the Angel and Our Lady are doing, namely, the Angel doing his duty as ambassador, and Our Lady humbling herself and giving thanks to the Divine Majesty; and then to reflect in order to draw some profit from each of these things.

Colloquy. At the end a Colloquy is to be made, thinking what I ought to say to the Three Divine Persons, or to the Eternal Word incarnate, or to our Mother and Lady, asking according to what I feel in me, in order more to follow and imitate Our Lord, so lately incarnate.

I will say an OUR FATHER.

THE SECOND CONTEMPLATION

Is On The Nativity

Prayer. The usual Preparatory Prayer.

First Prelude. The first Prelude is the narrative and it will be here how Our Lady went forth from Nazareth, about nine months with child, as can be piously meditated,[**9**] seated on an ass, and accompanied by Joseph and a maid, taking an ox, to go to Bethlehem to pay the tribute which Caesar imposed on all those lands (p. **135**).

Second Prelude. The second, a composition, seeing the place. It will be here to see with the sight of the imagination the road from Nazareth to Bethlehem; considering the length and the breadth, and whether such road is level or through valleys or over hills; likewise looking at the place or cave of the Nativity,[**10**] how large, how small, how low, how high, and how it was prepared.

Third Prelude. The third will be the same, and in the same form, as in the preceding Contemplation.

First Point. The first Point is to see the persons; that is, to see Our Lady and Joseph and the maid, and, after His Birth, the Child Jesus, I making myself a poor creature and a wretch of an unworthy slave, looking at them and serving them in their needs, with all possible respect and reverence, as if I found myself present;

and then to reflect on myself in order to draw some profit.

Second Point. The second, to look, mark and contemplate what they are saying, and, reflecting on myself, to draw some profit.

Third Point. The third, to look and consider what they are doing, as going a journey and laboring, that the Lord may be born in the greatest poverty; and as a termination of so many labors – of hunger, of thirst, of heat and of cold, of injuries and affronts – that He may die on the Cross; and all this for me: then reflecting, to draw some spiritual profit.

Colloquy. I will finish with a Colloquy as in the preceding Contemplation, and with an OUR FATHER

THE THIRD CONTEMPLATION

Will Be A Repetition Of The First And Second Exercise

After the Preparatory Prayer and the three Preludes, the repetition of the first and second Exercise will be made, noting always some more principal parts, where the person has felt some knowledge, consolation or desolation, making likewise one Colloquy at the end, and saying an OUR FATHER.

In this repetition, and in all the following, the same order of proceeding will be taken as was taken in the repetitions of the First Week, changing the matter and keeping the form.

THE FOURTH CONTEMPLATION

Will Be A Repetition Of The First And Second

In the same way as was done in the above-mentioned repetition.

THE FIFTH CONTEMPLATION

Will Be To Bring The Five Senses On The First And Second Contemplation

Prayer. After the Preparatory Prayer and the three Preludes, it is helpful to pass the five senses of the imagination through the first and second Contemplation, in the following way:

First Point. The first Point is to see the persons with the sight of the imagination, meditating and contemplating in particular the details about them and drawing some profit from the sight.

Second Point. The second, to hear with the hearing what they are, or might be, talking about and, reflecting on oneself, to draw some profit from it.

Third Point. The third, to smell and to taste with the smell and the taste the infinite fragrance and sweetness of the Divinity, of the soul, and of its virtues, and of all, according to the person who is being contemplated; reflecting on oneself and drawing profit from it.

Fourth Point. The fourth, to touch with the touch, as for instance, to embrace and kiss the places where such persons put their feet and sit, always seeing to my drawing profit from it.

Colloquy. One has to finish with one Colloquy as in the first and second Contemplation, and with an OUR FATHER.

First Note. The first note is to remark for all this and the other following Weeks, that I have only to read the Mystery of the Contemplation which I have immediately to make, so that at any time I read no Mystery which I have not to make that day or at that hour, in order that the consideration of one Mystery may not hinder the consideration of the other.

Second Note. The second: The first Exercise, on the Incarnation, will be made at midnight; the second at dawn; the third at the hour of Mass; the fourth at the hour of Vespers, and the fifth before the hour of supper, being for the space of one hour in each one of the five Exercises; and the same order will be taken in all the following.

Third Note. The third: It is to be remarked that if the person who is making the Exercises is old or weak, or, although strong, has become in some way less strong from the First Week, it is better for him in this Second Week, at least sometimes, not rising at midnight, to make one Contemplation in the morning, and another at the hour of Mass, and another before dinner, and one repetition on them at the hour of Vespers, and then the Application of the Senses before supper.

Fourth Note. The fourth: In this Second Week, out of all the ten Additions which were mentioned in the First Week, the second, the sixth, the seventh and in part the tenth have to be changed.

In the second it will be, immediately on waking up, to put before me the contemplation which I have to make, desiring to know more the Eternal Word incarnate, in order to serve and to follow Him more.

The sixth will be to bring frequently to memory the Life and Mysteries of Christ our Lord, from His Incarnation down to the place or Mystery which I am engaged in contemplating.

The seventh will be, that one should manage as to keeping darkness or light, making use of good weather or bad, according as he feels that it can profit and help him to find what the person desires who is exercising himself.

And in the tenth Addition, he who is exercising himself ought to manage himself according to the Mysteries which he is contemplating; because some demand penance and others not.

All the ten Additions, then, are to be made with great care.

Fifth Note. The fifth note: In all the Exercises, except in that of midnight and in that of the morning, the equivalent of the second Addition will be taken in the following way: – Immediately on recollecting that it is the time of the Exercise which I have to make, before I go, putting before myself where I am going and before Whom, and summarizing a little the Exercise which I have to make, and then making the third Addition, I will enter into the Exercise.

THE SECOND DAY

Second Day. For first and second Contemplation to take the Presentation in the Temple (p. **137**) and the Flight to Egypt as into exile (p. **138**), and on these two Contemplations will be made two repetitions and the Application of the Five Senses to them, in the same way as was done the preceding day.

Note. Sometimes, although the one who is exercising himself is strong and disposed, it helps to make a change, from this second day up to the fourth inclusively, in order better to find what he desires, taking only one Contemplation at daybreak, and another at the hour of Mass, and to repeat on them at the hour of Vespers and apply the senses before supper.

THE THIRD DAY

Third Day. How the Child Jesus was obedient to His Parents at Nazareth (p. **139**), and how afterwards they found Him in the Temple (p. **140**), and so then to make the two repetitions and apply the five senses.

PREAMBLE TO CONSIDER STATES

First Preamble. The example which Christ our Lord, being under obedience to His parents, has given us for the first state, – which consists in the observance of the Commandments – having been now considered; and likewise for the second, – which is that of evangelical perfection, – when He remained in the Temple, leaving His adoptive father and His natural Mother, to attend to the pure service of His eternal Father; we will begin, at the same time contemplating His life, to investigate and to ask in what life or state His Divine Majesty wants to be served by us.

And so, for some introduction of it, we will, in the first Exercise following, see the intention of Christ our Lord, and, on the contrary, that of the enemy of human nature, and how we ought to dispose ourselves in order to come to perfection in whatever state of life God our Lord would give us to choose.

THE FOURTH DAY

Meditation On Two Standards

The one of Christ, our Commander-in-chief and Lord; the other of Lucifer, mortal enemy of our human nature.

Prayer. The usual Preparatory Prayer.

First Prelude. The First Prelude is the narrative. It will be here how Christ calls and wants all under His standard; and Lucifer, on the contrary, under his.

Second Prelude. The second, a composition, seeing the place. It will be here to see a great field of all that region of Jerusalem, where the supreme Commander-in-chief of the good is Christ our Lord; another field in the region of Babylon, where the chief of the enemy is Lucifer.

Third Prelude. The third, to ask for what I want: and it will be here to ask for knowledge of the deceits of the bad chief and help to guard myself against them, and for knowledge of the true life which the supreme and true Captain shows and grace to imitate Him.

First Point. The first Point is to imagine as if the chief of all the enemy seated himself in that great field of Babylon, as in a great [**11**] chair of fire and smoke, in shape horrible and terrifying.

Second Point. The second, to consider how he issues a summons to innumerable demons and how he scatters them, some to one city and others to another, and so through all the world, not omitting any provinces, places, states, nor any persons in particular.

Third Point. The third, to consider the discourse which he makes them, and how he tells them to cast out nets and chains; that they have first to tempt with a longing for riches – as he is accustomed to do in most cases [**12**] – that men may more easily come to vain honor of the world, and then to vast pride. So that the first step shall be that of riches; the second, that of honor; the third, that of pride; and from these three steps he draws on to all the other vices.

So, on the contrary, one has to imagine as to the supreme and true Captain, Who is Christ our Lord.

First Point. The first Point is to consider how Christ our Lord puts Himself in a great field of that region of Jerusalem, in lowly place, beautiful and attractive.

Second Point. The second, to consider how the Lord of all the world chooses so many persons – Apostles, Disciples, etc., – and sends them through all the world spreading His sacred doctrine through all states and conditions of persons.

Third Point. The third, to consider the discourse which Christ our Lord makes to all His servants and friends whom He sends on this expedition, recommending them to want to help all, by bringing them first to the highest spiritual poverty, and – if His Divine Majesty would be served and would want to choose them – no less to actual poverty; the second is to be of contumely and contempt; because from these two things humility follows. So that there are to be three steps; the first, poverty against riches; the second, contumely or contempt against worldly honor; the third, humility against pride. And from these three steps let them induce to all the other virtues.

First Colloquy. One Colloquy to Our Lady, that she may get me grace from Her Son and Lord that I may be received under His standard; and first in the highest spiritual poverty, and – if His Divine Majesty would be served and would want to choose and receive me – not less in actual poverty; second, in suffering contumely and injuries, to imitate Him more in them, if only I can suffer them without the sin of any person, or displeasure of His Divine Majesty; and with that a HAIL MARY.

Second Colloquy. I will ask the same of the Son, that He may get it for me of the Father; and with that say the SOUL OF CHRIST.

Third Colloquy. I will ask the same of the Father, that He may grant it to me; and say an OUR FATHER.

Note. This Exercise will be made at midnight and then a second time in the morning, and two repetitions of this same will be made at the hour of Mass and at the hour of Vespers, always finishing with the three Colloquies, to Our Lady, to the Son, and to the Father; and that on The Pairs which follows, at the hour before supper.

THE SAME FOURTH DAY LET MEDITATION BE MADE ON

Three Pairs Of Men In Order To Embrace What Is Best

Prayer. The usual Preparatory Prayer.

First Prelude. The first Prelude is the narrative, which is of three pairs of men, and each one of them has acquired ten thousand ducats, not solely or as they ought [**13**] for God's love, and all want to save themselves and find in peace God our Lord, ridding themselves of the weight and hindrance to it which they have in the attachment for the thing acquired.

Second Prelude. The second, a composition, seeing the place. It will be here to see myself, how I stand before God our Lord and all His Saints, to desire and know what is more pleasing to His Divine Goodness.

Third Prelude. The third, to ask for what I want. Here it will be to ask grace to choose what is more to the glory of His Divine Majesty and the salvation of my soul.

First Pair. The first Pair would want to rid themselves of the attachment which they have to the thing acquired, in order to find in peace God our Lord, and be able to save themselves, and they do not place the means up to the hour of death.

Second Pair. The second want to rid themselves of the attachment, but want so to rid themselves of it as to remain with the thing acquired, so that God should come where they want, and they do not decide to leave it in order to go to God, although it would be the best state for them

Third Pair. The third want to rid themselves of the attachment, but want so to rid themselves of it that they have even no liking for it, to keep the thing acquired or not to keep it, but only want to want it or not want it according as God our Lord will put in their will and as will appear to them better for the service and praise of His Divine Majesty; and meanwhile they want to reckon that they quit it all in attachment, forcing themselves not to want that or any other thing, unless only the service of God our Lord move them: so that the desire of being better able to serve God our Lord moves them to take the thing or leave it.

Three Colloquies. I will make the same three Colloquies which were made in the Contemplation preceding, on the Two Standards.

Note. It is to be noted that when we feel a tendency or repugnance against actual poverty, when we are not indifferent to poverty or riches, it is very helpful, in order to crush such disordered tendency, to ask in the Colloquies (although it be against the flesh) that the Lord should choose one to actual poverty, and that one wants, asks and begs it, if only it be the service and praise of His Divine Goodness.

THE FIFTH DAY

Fifth Day. Contemplation on the Departure of Christ our Lord from Nazareth to the River Jordan, and how He was baptized (p. **140**).

First Note. This Contemplation will be made once at midnight and a second time in the morning, and two repetitions on it at the hour of Mass and Vespers, and the five senses will be applied on it before supper; in each of these five Exercises, putting first the usual Preparatory Prayer and the three Preludes, as all this was explained in the Contemplation of the Incarnation and of the Nativity; and finishing with the three Colloquies of the three Pairs, or according to the note which follows after the Pairs.

Second Note. The Particular Examen, after dinner and after supper, will be made on the faults and negligences about the Exercises and Additions of this day; and so in the days that follow.

THE SIXTH DAY

Sixth Day. Contemplation how Christ our Lord went forth from the River Jordan to the Desert inclusive, taking the same form in everything as on the fifth.

THE SEVENTH DAY

Seventh Day. How St. Andrew and others followed Christ our Lord (p. **142**).

THE EIGHTH DAY

Eighth Day. On the Sermon on the Mount, which is on the Eight Beatitudes (P. **144**).

THE NINTH DAY

Ninth Day. How Christ our Lord appeared to His disciples on the waves of the sea (p. **145**).

THE TENTH DAY

Tenth Day. How the Lord preached in the [**14**] Temple (p. **151**).

THE ELEVENTH DAY

Eleventh Day. On the raising of Lazarus (p. **149**).

THE TWELFTH DAY

Twelfth Day. On Palm Sunday (p. **151**).

First Note. The first note is that in the Contemplations of this Second Week, according to the time each one wants to spend, or according as he gets profit, he can lengthen or shorten: if he lengthens, taking the Mysteries of the Visitation of Our Lady to St. Elizabeth, the Shepherds, the Circumcision of the Child Jesus, and the Three Kings, and so of others; and if he shortens, he can even omit some of those which are set down. Because this is to give an introduction and way to contemplate better and more completely afterwards.

Second Note. The second: The matter of the Elections will be begun from the Contemplation on Nazareth to the Jordan, taken inclusively, which is the fifth day, as is explained in the following.

Third Note. The third: Before entering on the Elections, that a man may get attachment to the true doctrine of Christ our Lord, it is very helpful to consider and mark the following three Manners of Humility, reflecting on them occasionally through all the day, and also making the Colloquies, as will be said later.

First Humility. The first manner of Humility is necessary for eternal salvation; namely, that I so lower and so humble myself, as much as is possible to me, that in everything I obey the law of God, so that, even if they made me lord of all the created things in this world, nor for my own temporal life, I would not be in deliberation about breaking a Commandment, whether Divine or human, which binds me under mortal sin.

Second Humility. The second is more perfect Humility than the first; namely, if I find myself at such a stage that I do not want, and feel no inclination to have, riches rather than poverty, to want honor rather than dishonor, to desire a long rather than a short life – the service of God our Lord and the salvation of my soul being equal; and so not for all creation, nor because they would take away my life, would I be in deliberation about committing a venial sin.

Third Humility. The third is most perfect Humility; namely, when – including the first and second, and the praise and glory of the Divine Majesty being equal – in order to imitate and be more actually like Christ our Lord, I want and choose poverty with Christ poor rather than riches, opprobrium with Christ replete with it rather than honors; and to desire to be rated as worthless and a fool for Christ, Who first was held as such, rather than wise or prudent in this world.

Note. So, it is very helpful for whoever desires to get this third Humility, to make the three already mentioned Colloquies of THE PAIRS, asking that Our Lord would be pleased to choose him to this third greater and better Humility, in order more to imitate and serve Him, if it be equal or greater service and praise to His Divine Majesty.

PRELUDE FOR MAKING ELECTION

First Point. In every good election, as far as depends on us, the eye of our intention ought to be simple, only looking at what we are created for, namely, the praise of God our Lord and the salvation of our soul. And so I ought to choose whatever I do, that it may help me for the end for which I am created, not ordering or bringing the end to the means, but the means to the end: as it happens that many choose first to marry – which is a means – and secondarily to serve God our Lord in the married life – which service of God is the end. So, too, there are others who first want to have benefices, and then to serve God in them. So that those do not go straight to God, but want God to come straight to their disordered tendencies, and consequently they make a means of the end, and an end of the means. So that what they had to take first, they take last; because first we have to set as our aim the wanting to serve God, – which is the end, – and secondarily, to take a benefice, or to marry, if it is more suitable to us, – which is the means for the end. So, nothing ought to move me to take such means or to deprive myself of them, except only the service and praise of God our Lord and the eternal salvation of my soul.

TO GET KNOWLEDGE AS TO WHAT MATTERS AN ELECTION OUGHT TO BE MADE ABOUT, AND IT CONTAINS FOUR POINTS AND ONE NOTE

First Point. The first Point: It is necessary that everything about which we want to make an election should be indifferent, or good, in itself, and should be allowed within our Holy Mother the hierarchical Church, and not bad nor opposed to her.

Second Point. Second: There are some things which fall under unchangeable election, such as are the priesthood, marriage, etc. There are others which fall under an election that can be changed, such as are to take benefices or leave them, to take temporal goods or rid oneself of them.

Third Point. Third: In the unchangeable Election which has already been once made – such as marriage, the priesthood, etc. – there is nothing more to choose, because one cannot release himself; only it is to be seen to that if one have not made his election duly and ordinately and without disordered tendencies, repenting let him see to living a good life in his election. It does not appear that this election is a Divine vocation,[**15**] as being an election out of order and awry. Many err in this, setting up a perverse or bad election as a Divine [**16**] vocation; for every Divine vocation is always pure and clear, without mixture of flesh, or of any other inordinate tendency.

Fourth Point. Fourth: If some one has duly and ordinately made election of things which are under election that can be changed, and has not yielded to flesh or world, there is no reason for his making election anew, but let him perfect himself as much as he can in that already chosen.

Note. It is to be remarked that if such election that can be changed was not made sincerely and well in order, then it helps to make the election duly, if one has a desire that fruits notable and very pleasing to God our Lord should come from him.

THREE TIMES

FOR MAKING, IN ANY ONE OF THEM, A SOUND AND GOOD ELECTION

First Time. The first time is, when God our Lord so moves and attracts the will, that without doubting, or being able to doubt, such devout soul follows what is shown it, as St. Paul and St. Matthew did in following Christ our Lord.

Second Time. The second, when enough light and knowledge is received by experience of consolations and desolations, and by the experience of the discernment of various spirits.

Third Time. The third time is quiet, when one considers, first, for what man is born – namely, to praise God our Lord and save his soul – and desiring this chooses as means a life or state within the limits of the Church, in order that he may be helped in the service of his Lord and the salvation of his soul.

I said time of quiet, when the soul is not acted on by various spirits, and uses its natural powers freely and tranquilly.

If election is not made in the first or the second time, two ways follow as to this third time for making it.

THE FIRST WAY

TO MAKE A SOUND AND GOOD ELECTION

It contains six Points.

First Point. The first Point is to put before me the thing on which I want to make election, such as an office or benefice, either to take or leave it; or any other thing whatever which falls under an election that can be changed.

Second Point. Second: It is necessary to keep as aim the end for which I am created, which is to praise God our Lord and save my soul, and, this supposed, to find myself indifferent, without any inordinate propensity; so that I be not more inclined or disposed to take the thing proposed than to leave it, nor more to leave it than to take it, but find myself as in the middle of a balance, to follow what I feel to be more for the glory and praise of God our Lord and the salvation of my soul.

Third Point. Third: To ask of God our Lord to be pleased to move my will and put in my soul what I ought to do regarding the thing proposed, so as to promote more His praise and glory; discussing well and faithfully with my intellect, and choosing agreeably to His most holy pleasure and will.

Fourth Point. Fourth: To consider, reckoning up, how many advantages and utilities follow for me from holding the proposed office or benefice for only the praise of God our Lord and the salvation of my soul, and, to consider likewise, on the contrary, the disadvantages and dangers which there are in having it. Doing the same in the second part, that is, looking at the advantages and utilities there are in not having it, and likewise, on the contrary, the disadvantages and dangers in not having the same.

Fifth Point. Fifth: After I have thus discussed and reckoned up on all sides about the thing proposed, to look where reason more inclines: and so, according to the greater inclination of reason, and not according to any inclination of sense, deliberation should be made on the thing proposed.

Sixth Point. Sixth, such election, or deliberation, made, the person who has made it ought to go with much diligence to prayer before God our Lord and offer Him such election, that His Divine Majesty may be pleased to receive and confirm it, if it is to His greater service and praise.

THE SECOND WAY

TO MAKE A GOOD AND SOUND ELECTION

It contains four Rules and one Note.

First Rule. The first is that that love which moves me and makes me choose such thing should descend from above, from the love of God, so that he who chooses feel first in himself that that love, more or less, which he has for the thing which he chooses, is only for his Creator and Lord.

Second Rule. The second, to set before me a man whom I have never seen nor known, and I [**17**] desiring all his perfection, to consider what I would tell him to do and elect for the greater glory of God our Lord, and the greater perfection of his soul, and I, doing likewise, to keep the rule which I set for the other.

Third Rule. The third, to consider, as if I were at the point of death, the form and measure which I would then want to have kept in the way of the present election, and regulating myself by that election, let me make my decision in everything.

Fourth Rule. The fourth, looking and considering how I shall find myself on the Day of Judgment, to think how I would then want to have[**18**] deliberated about the present matter, and to take now the rule which I would then wish to have kept, in order that I may then find myself in entire pleasure and joy.

Note. The above-mentioned rules for my eternal salvation and peace having been taken, I will make my election and offering to God our Lord, conformably to the sixth Point of the First Way of making election.

TO AMEND AND REFORM ONE'S OWN LIFE

AND STATE

It is to be noted that as to those who are settled in ecclesiastical office or in matrimony – whether they abound much or not in temporal goods – when they have no opportunity or have not a very prompt will to make election about the things which fall under an election that can be changed, it is very helpful, in place of making election, to give them a form and way to amend and reform each his own life and state. That is, putting his creation, life and state for the glory and praise of God our Lord and the salvation of his own soul, to come and arrive at this end, he ought to consider much and ponder through the Exercises and Ways of Election, as has been explained, how large a house and household he ought to keep, how he ought to rule and govern it, how he ought to teach and instruct it by word and by example; likewise of his means, how much he ought to take for his household and house; and how much to dispense to the poor and to other pious objects, not wanting nor seeking any other thing except in all and through all the greater praise and glory of God our Lord.

For let each one think that he will benefit himself in all spiritual things in proportion as he goes out of his self-love, will and interest.

IX. Third Week

FIRST DAY

THE FIRST CONTEMPLATION AT MIDNIGHT IS

HOW CHRIST OUR LORD WENT FROM BETHANY TO JERUSALEM TO THE LAST SUPPER INCLUSIVELY

(p. **152**); and it contains the Preparatory Prayer, three Preludes, six Points and one Colloquy.

Prayer. The usual Preparatory Prayer.

First Prelude. The first Prelude is to bring to memory the narrative; which is here how Christ our Lord sent two Disciples from Bethany to Jerusalem to prepare the Supper, and then He Himself went there with the other Disciples; and how, after having eaten the Paschal Lamb, and having supped, He washed their feet and gave His most Holy Body and Precious Blood to His Disciples, and made them a discourse, after Judas went to sell his Lord.

Second Prelude. The second, a composition, seeing the place. It will be here to consider the road from Bethany to Jerusalem, whether broad, whether narrow, whether level, etc.; likewise the place of the Supper, whether large, whether small, whether of one kind or whether of another.

Third Prelude. The third, to ask for what I want. It will be here grief, feeling and confusion because for my sins the Lord is going to the Passion.

First Point. The first Point is to see the persons of the Supper, and, reflecting on myself, to see to drawing some profit from them.

Second Point. The second, to hear what they are talking about, and likewise to draw some profit from it.

Third Point. The third, to look at what they are doing, and draw some profit.

Fourth Point. The fourth, to consider that which Christ our Lord is suffering in His Humanity,[**19**] or wants to suffer, according to the passage which is being contemplated, and here to commence with much vehemence and to force myself to grieve, be sad and weep, and so to labor through the other points which follow.

Fifth Point. The fifth, to consider how the Divinity hides Itself, that is, how It could destroy Its enemies and does not do it, and how It leaves the most sacred Humanity to suffer so very cruelly.

Sixth Point. The sixth, to consider how He suffers all this for my sins, etc.; and what I ought to do and suffer for Him.

Colloquy. I will finish with a Colloquy to Christ our Lord, and, at the end, with an OUR FATHER.

Note. It is to be noted, as was explained before and in part, that in the Colloquies I ought to discuss and ask according to the subject matter, that is, according as I find myself tempted or consoled, and according as I desire to have one virtue or another, as I want to dispose of myself in one direction or another, as I want to grieve or rejoice at the thing which I am contemplating; in fine, asking that which I more efficaciously desire as to any particular things. And in this way I can make one Colloquy only, to Christ our Lord, or, if the matter or devotion move me, three Colloquies, one to the Mother, another to the Son, another to the Father, in the same form as was said in the SECOND WEEK, in the meditation of the THREE PAIRS, with the Note which follows THE PAIRS.

SECOND DAY

SECOND CONTEMPLATION IN THE MORNING

FROM THE SUPPER TO THE GARDEN INCLUSIVELY

Prayer. The usual Preparatory Prayer

First Prelude. The first Prelude is the narrative and it will be here how Christ our Lord went down with His eleven Disciples from Mount Sion, where He made the Supper, to the Valley of Josaphat. Leaving the eight in a part of the Valley and the other three in a part of the Garden, and putting Himself in prayer, He sweats sweat as drops of blood,[**20**] and after He prayed three times to the Father and wakened His three Disciples, and after the enemies at His voice fell down, Judas giving Him the kiss of peace, and St. Peter cutting off the ear of Malchus, and Christ putting it in its place; being taken as a malefactor, they lead Him down the valley, and then up the side, to the house of Annas.

Second Prelude. The second is to see the place. It will be here to consider the road from Mount Sion to the Valley of Josaphat, and likewise the Garden, whether wide, whether large, whether of one kind, whether of another.

Third Prelude. The third is to ask for what I want. It belongs to the Passion to ask for grief with Christ in grief, anguish with Christ in anguish, tears and interior pain at such great pain which Christ suffered for me.

First Note. In this second Contemplation, after the Preparatory Prayer is made, with the three Preludes already mentioned, the same form of proceeding will be kept through the Points and Colloquy as was kept in the first Contemplation, on the Supper.

And at the hour of Mass and Vespers two repetitions will be made on the first and second Contemplation, and then, before supper, the senses will be applied on the two above-said Contemplations, always prefixing the Preparatory Prayer and the three Preludes, according to the subject matter, in the same form as was said and explained in the SECOND WEEK.

Second Note. According as age, disposition and physical condition help the person who is exercising himself, he will make each day the five Exercises or fewer.

Third Note. In this THIRD WEEK the second and sixth Additions will in part be changed.

The second will be, immediately on awaking, to set before me where I am going and to what, and summing up a little the contemplation which I want to make, according as the Mystery shall be, to force myself, while I am getting up and dressing, to be sad and grieve over such great grief and such great suffering of Christ our Lord.

The sixth will be changed, so as not to try to bring joyful thoughts, although good and holy, as, for instance, are those on the Resurrection and on heavenly glory, but rather to draw myself to grief and to pain and anguish, bringing to mind frequently the labors, fatigues and pains of Christ our Lord, which He suffered from the moment when He was born up to the Mystery of the Passion in which I find myself at present.

Fourth Note. The Particular Examen on the Exercises and present Additions, will be made as it was made in the past Week.

Second Day. The second day at midnight, the Contemplation will be from the Garden to the house of Annas inclusive (P. **154**), and in the morning from the house of Annas to the house of Caiphas inclusive (P. **155**), and then the two repetitions and the application of the senses, as has been already said.

Third Day. The third day, at midnight, from the house of Caiphas to Pilate, inclusive (p. **155**); and in the morning, from Pilate to Herod inclusive (p. **156**); and then the repetitions and senses, in the same form as has been already said.

Fourth Day. The fourth day, at midnight, from Herod to Pilate (p. **157**), doing and contemplating up to half through the Mysteries of the same house of Pilate, and then, in the Exercise of the morning, the other Mysteries which remained of the same house; and the repetitions and the senses, as has been said.

Fifth Day. The fifth day, at midnight, from the house of Pilate up to the Crucifixion (p. **158**), and in the morning from His being raised on the Cross until

He expired (p. **158**), then the two repetitions, and the senses.

Sixth Day. The sixth day, at midnight, from the Descent from the Cross to the Tomb, exclusive (p. **159**) and in the morning from the Tomb, inclusive, to the house where Our Lady was, after her Son was buried.

Seventh Day. The seventh day, a Contemplation on the whole Passion together, in the Exercise of midnight and of the morning, and in place of the two repetitions and of the senses one will consider all that day, as frequently as he can, how the most holy Body of Christ our Lord remained separated and apart from the Soul: and where and how It remained buried. Likewise, one will consider the loneliness of Our Lady, whose grief and fatigue were so great: then, on the other side, the loneliness of the Disciples.

Note. It is to be noted that whoever wants to dwell more on the Passion, has to take in each Contemplation fewer Mysteries; that is to say, in the first Contemplation, the Supper only; in the second, the Washing of the Feet; in the third, the giving of the Blessed Sacrament to them; in the fourth, the discourse which Christ made to them; and so through the other Contemplations and Mysteries.

Likewise, after having finished the Passion, let him take for an entire day the half of the whole Passion, and the second day the other half, and the third day the whole Passion.

On the contrary, whoever would want to shorten more in the Passion, let him take at midnight the Supper, in the morning the Garden, at the hour of Mass the house of Annas, at the hour of Vespers the house of Caiphas, in place of the hour before supper the house of Pilate; so that, not making repetitions, nor the Application of the Senses, he make each day five distinct Exercises, and in each Exercise take a distinct Mystery of Christ our Lord. And after thus finishing the whole Passion, he can, another day, do all the Passion together in one Exercise, or in different ones, as it will seem to him that he will be better able to help himself.

RULES TO PUT ONESELF IN ORDER FOR THE FUTURE AS TO EATING

First Rule. The first rule is that it is well to abstain less from bread, because it is not a food as to which the appetite is used to act so inordinately, or to which temptation urges as in the case of the other foods.

Second Rule. The second: Abstinence appears more convenient as to drinking, than as to eating bread. So, one ought to look much what is helpful to him, in order to admit it, and what does him harm, in order to discard it.

Third Rule. The third: As to foods, one ought to have the greatest and most entire abstinence, because as the appetite is more ready to act inordinately, so temptation is more ready in making trial, on this head. And so abstinence in foods, to avoid disorder, can be kept in two ways, one by accustoming oneself to eat coarse foods; the other, if one takes delicate foods, by taking them in small quantity.

Fourth Rule. The fourth: Guarding against falling into sickness, the more a man leaves off from what is suitable, the more quickly he will reach the mean which he ought to keep in his eating and drinking; for two reasons: the first, because by so helping and disposing himself, he will many times experience more the interior knowledge, consolations and Divine inspirations to show him the mean which is proper for him; the second, because if the person sees himself in such abstinence not with so great corporal strength or disposition for the Spiritual Exercises, he will easily come to judge what is more suitable to his bodily support.

Fifth Rule. The fifth: While the person is eating, let him consider as if he saw Christ our Lord eating with His Apostles, and how He drinks and how He looks and how He speaks; and let him see to imitating Him. So that the principal part of the intellect shall occupy itself in the consideration of Christ our Lord, and the lesser part in the support of the body; because in this way he will get greater system and order as to how he ought to behave and manage himself.

Sixth Rule. The sixth: Another time, while he is eating, he can take another consideration, either on the life of Saints, or on some pious Contemplation, or on some spiritual affair which he has to do, because, being intent on such thing, he will take less delight and feeling in the corporal food.

Seventh Rule. The seventh: Above all, let him guard against all his soul being intent on what he is eating, and in eating let him not go hurriedly, through appetite, but be master of himself, as well in the manner of eating as in the quantity which he eats.

Eighth Rule. The eighth: To avoid disorder, it is very helpful, after dinner or after supper, or at another hour when one feels no appetite for eating, to decide with oneself for the coming dinner or supper, and so on, each day, the quantity which it is suitable that he should eat. Beyond this let him not go because of any appetite or temptation, but rather, in order to conquer more all inordinate appetite and temptation of the enemy, if he is tempted to eat more, let him eat less.

X. Fourth Week

THE FIRST CONTEMPLATION

HOW CHRIST OUR LORD APPEARED TO OUR LADY

Prayer. The usual Preparatory Prayer.

First Prelude. The first Prelude is the narrative, which is here how, after Christ expired on the Cross, and the Body, always united with the Divinity, remained separated from the Soul, the blessed Soul, likewise united with the Divinity, went down to Hell, and taking from there the just souls, and coming to the Sepulchre and being risen, He appeared to His Blessed Mother in Body and in Soul.

Second Prelude. The second, a composition, seeing the place; which will be here to see the arrangement of the Holy Sepulchre and the place or house of Our Lady, looking at its parts in particular; likewise the room, the oratory, etc.

Third Prelude. The third, to ask for what I want, and it will be here to ask for grace to rejoice and be glad intensely at so great glory and joy of Christ our Lord.

First Point, Second Point, and Third Point. Let the first, second and third Points be the same usual ones which we took in the Supper of Christ our Lord.

Fourth Point. The fourth, to consider how the Divinity, which seemed to hide Itself in the Passion, now appears and shows Itself so marvellously in the most holy Resurrection by Its true and most holy effects.

Fifth Point. The fifth is to consider the office of consoling which Christ our Lord bears, and to compare how friends are accustomed to console friends.

Colloquy. I will finish with a Colloquy, or Colloquies, according to the subject matter, and an OUR FATHER.

First Note. In the following Contemplations let one go on through all the Mysteries of the Resurrection, in the manner which follows below, up to the Ascension inclusive, taking and keeping in the rest the same form and manner in all the Week of the Resurrection which was taken in all the Week of the Passion. So that, for this first Contemplation, on the Resurrection, let one guide himself as to the Preludes according to the subject matter; and as to the five Points, let them be the same; and let the Additions which are below be the same; and so in all which remains, he can guide himself by the method of the Week of the Passion, as in repetitions, the five Senses, in shortening or lengthening the Mysteries.

Second Note. The second note: Commonly in this FOURTH WEEK, it is more suitable than in the other three past to make four Exercises, and not five: the first, immediately on rising in the morning; the second, at the hour of Mass, or before dinner, in place of the first repetition; the third, at the hour of Vespers, in place of the second repetition; the fourth, before supper, bringing the five Senses on the three Exercises of the same day, noting and lingering on the more principal parts, and where one has felt greater spiritual movements and relish.

Third Note. The third: Though in all the Contemplations so many Points were given in certain number – as three, or five, etc., the person who is contemplating can set more or fewer Points, according as he finds it better for him. For which it is very helpful, before entering on the Contemplation, to conjecture and mark in certain number the Points which he is to take.

Fourth Note. In this FOURTH WEEK, in all the ten Additions the second, the sixth, the seventh and the tenth are to be changed.

The second will be, immediately on awaking, to put before me the Contemplation which I have to make, wanting to arouse feeling and be glad at the great joy and gladness of Christ our Lord.

The sixth, to bring to memory and think of things that move to spiritual pleasure, gladness and joy, as of heavenly glory.

The seventh, to use light or temporal comforts – as, in summer, the coolness; and in winter, the sun or heat – as far as the soul thinks or conjectures that it can help it to be joyful in its Creator and Redeemer.

The tenth: in place of penance, let one regard temperance and all moderation; except it is question of precepts of fasting or of abstinence which the Church commands; because those are always to be fulfilled, if there is no just impediment.

CONTEMPLATION TO GAIN LOVE

Note. First, it is well to remark two things: the first is that love ought to be put more in deeds than in words.

The second, love consists in interchange between the two parties; that is to say in the lover's giving and communicating to the beloved what he has or out of what he has or can; and so, on the contrary, the beloved to the lover. So that if the one has knowledge, he give to the one who has it not. The same of honors, of riches; and so the one to the other.

CONTEMPLATION TO GAIN LOVE

Prayer. The usual Prayer.

First Prelude. The first Prelude is a composition, which is here to see how I am standing before God our Lord, and of the Angels and of the Saints interceding for me.

Second Prelude. The second, to ask for what I want. It will be here to ask for interior knowledge of so great good received, in order that being entirely grateful, I may be able in all to love and serve His Divine Majesty.

First Point. The First Point is, to bring to memory the benefits received, of Creation, Redemption and particular gifts, pondering with much feeling how much God our Lord has done for me, and how much He has given me of what He has, and then the same Lord desires to give me Himself as much as He can, according to His Divine ordination.

And with this to reflect on myself, considering with much reason and justice, what I ought on my side to offer and give to His Divine Majesty, that is to say, everything that is mine, and myself with it, as one who makes an offering with much feeling:

Take, Lord, and receive all my liberty, my memory, my intellect, and all my will – all that I have and possess. Thou gavest it to me: to Thee, Lord, I return it! All is Thine, dispose of it according to all Thy will. Give me Thy love and grace, for this is enough for me.

Second Point. The second, to look how God dwells in creatures, in the elements, giving them being, in the plants vegetating, in the animals feeling in them, in men giving them to understand:[**21**] and so in me, giving me being, animating me, giving me sensation and making me to understand;[**22**] likewise making a temple of me, being created to the likeness and image of His Divine Majesty; reflecting as much on myself in the way which is said in the first Point, or in another which I feel to be better. In the same manner will be done on each Point which follows.

Third Point. The third, to consider how God works and labors for me in all things created on the face of the earth – that is, behaves like one who labors – as in the heavens, elements, plants, fruits, cattle, etc., giving them being, preserving them, giving them vegetation and sensation, etc.

Then to reflect on myself.

Fourth Point. The fourth, to look how all the good things and gifts descend from above, as my poor power from the supreme and infinite power from above;

and so justice, goodness, pity, mercy, etc.; as from the sun descend the rays, from the fountain the waters, etc.

Then to finish reflecting on myself, as has been said.

I will end with a Colloquy and an OUR FATHER.

XI. Three Methods Of Prayer

AND FIRST ON THE COMMANDMENTS

FIRST METHOD

The first Method of Prayer is on the Ten Commandments, and on the Seven Deadly Sins, on the Three Powers of the Soul and on the Five Bodily Senses. This method of prayer is meant more to give form, method and exercises, how the soul may prepare itself and benefit in them, and that the prayer may be acceptable, rather than to give any form or way of praying.

I. The Ten Commandments

First let the equivalent of the second Addition of the SECOND WEEK be made; that is, before entering on the prayer, let the spirit rest a little, the person being seated or walking about, as may seem best to him, considering where he is going and to what. And this same addition will be made at the beginning of all Methods of Prayer.

Prayer. A Preparatory Prayer, as, for example, to ask grace of God our Lord that I may be able to know in what I have failed as to the Ten Commandments; and likewise to beg grace and help to amend in future, asking for perfect understanding of them, to keep them better and for the greater glory and praise of His Divine Majesty.

For the first Method of Prayer, it is well to consider and think on the First Commandment, how I have kept it and in what I have failed, keeping to the rule of spending the space of time one says the OUR FATHER and the HAIL MARY three times; and if in this time I find faults of mine, to ask pardon and forgiveness for them, and say an OUR FATHER. Let this same method be followed on each one of the Ten Commandments.

First Note. It is to be noted that when one comes to think on a Commandment on which he finds he has no habit of sinning, it is not necessary for him to delay so much time, but according as one finds in himself that he stumbles more or less on that Commandment so he ought to keep himself more or less on the consideration and examination of it. And the same is to be observed on the Deadly Sins.

Second Note. After having finished the discussion already mentioned on all the Commandments, accusing myself on them and asking grace and help to amend hereafter, I am to finish with a Colloquy to God our Lord, according to the subject matter.

II. On Deadly Sins

About the Seven Deadly Sins, after the Addition, let the Preparatory Prayer be made in the way already mentioned, only with the difference that the matter here is of sins that have to be avoided, and before of Commandments that have to be kept: and likewise let the order and rule already mentioned be kept, and the Colloquy.

In order to know better the faults committed in the Deadly Sins, let their contraries be looked at: and so, to avoid them better, let the person purpose and with holy exercises see to acquiring and keeping the seven virtues contrary to them.

III. On the Powers of the Soul

Way. On the three powers of the soul let the same order and rule be kept as on the Commandments, making its Addition, Preparatory Prayer and Colloquy.

IV. On the Bodily Senses

Way. About the five bodily senses the same order always will be kept, but changing their matter.

Note. Whoever wants to imitate Christ our Lord in the use of his senses, let him in the Preparatory Prayer recommend himself to His Divine Majesty, and after considering on each sense, say a HAIL MARY or an OUR FATHER.

And whoever wants to imitate Our Lady in the use of the senses, let him in the Preparatory Prayer recommend himself to her, that she may get him grace from Her Son and Lord for it; and after considering on each sense, say a HAIL MARY.

SECOND METHOD OF PRAYER

It is by contemplating the meaning of each word of the Prayer.

Addition. The same Addition which was in the First Method of Prayer will be in this second.

Prayer. The Preparatory Prayer will be made according to the person to whom the prayer is addressed.

Second Method of Prayer. The Second Method of Prayer is that the person, kneeling or seated, according to the greater disposition in which he finds himself and as more devotion accompanies him, keeping the eyes closed or fixed on one place, without going wandering with them, says FATHER, and is on the consideration of this word as long as he finds meanings, comparisons, relish and consolation in considerations pertaining to such word. And let him do in the same way on each word of the OUR FATHER, or of any other prayer which he wants to say in this way.

First Rule. The first Rule is that he will be an hour on the whole OUR FATHER in the manner already mentioned. Which finished, he will say a HAIL MARY, CREED, SOUL OF CHRIST, and HAIL, HOLY QUEEN, vocally or mentally, according to the usual way.

Second Rule. The Second Rule is that, should the person who is contemplating the OUR FATHER find in one word, or in two, matter so good to think over, and relish and consolation, let him not care to pass on, although the hour ends on what he finds. The hour finished, he will say the rest of the OUR FATHER in the usual way.

Third Rule. The third is that if on one word or two of the OUR FATHER one has lingered for a whole hour, when he will want to come back another day to the prayer, let him say the above-mentioned word, or the two, as he is accustomed; and on the word which immediately follows let him commence to contemplate, according as was said in the second Rule.

First Note. It is to be noted that, the OUR FATHER finished, in one or in many days, the same has to be done with the HAIL MARY and then with the other prayers, so that for some time one is always exercising himself in one of them.

Second Note. The second note is that, the prayer finished, turning, in few words, to the person to whom he has prayed, let him ask for the virtues or graces of which he feels he has most need.

THIRD METHOD OF PRAYER

It will be by rhythm.

Addition. The Addition will be the same as in the First and Second Methods of Prayer.

Prayer. The Preparatory Prayer will be as in the Second Method of Prayer.

Third Method of Prayer. The Third Method of Prayer is that with each breath in or out, one has to pray mentally, saying one word of the OUR FATHER, or of another prayer which is being recited: so that only one word be said between one breath and another, and while the time from one breath to another lasts, let attention be given chiefly to the meaning of such word, or to the person to whom he recites it, or to his own baseness, or to the difference from such great height to his own so great lowness. And in the same form and rule he will proceed on the other words of the OUR FATHER; and the other prayers, that is to say, the HAIL MARY, the SOUL OF CHRIST, the CREED, and the HAIL, HOLY QUEEN, he will make as he is accustomed.

First Rule. The First Rule is, on the other day, or at another hour, that he wants to pray, let him say the HAIL MARY in rhythm, and the other prayers as he is accustomed; and so on, going through the others.

Second Rule. The second is that whoever wants to dwell more on the prayer by rhythm, can say all the above-mentioned prayers or part of them, keeping the same order of the breath by rhythm, as has been explained.

XII. The Mysteries Of The Life Of Christ Our Lord

Note. It is to be noted in all the following Mysteries, that all the words which are inclosed in parentheses[**23**] are from the Gospel itself and not those which are outside.

And in each Mystery, for the most part, three Points will be found to meditate and contemplate on with greater ease.

OF THE ANNUNCIATION OF OUR LADY

St. Luke writes in the first Chapter [**26-39**].

First Point. The first Point is that the Angel St. Gabriel, saluting Our Lady, announced to her the Conception of Christ our Lord. "The Angel entering where Mary was, saluted her saying: `Hail full of grace. Thou shalt conceive in thy womb and shalt bring forth a son.'"

Second Point. The second, the Angel confirms what he said to Our Lady, telling of the conception of St. John Baptist, saying to her: "`And behold thy cousin Elizabeth hath conceived a son in her old age.'"

Third Point. The third, Our Lady answered the Angel: "`Behold the handmaid of the Lord: be it done to me according to thy word!'"

OF THE VISITATION OF OUR LADY TO ELIZABETH

St. Luke speaks in the first Chapter [**39-57**].

First Point. First: As Our Lady visited Elizabeth, St. John Baptist, being in his mother's womb, felt the visitation which Our Lady made. "And when Elizabeth heard the salutation of Our Lady, the infant leaped in her womb. And Elizabeth, full of the Holy Ghost, cried out with a loud voice, and said: `Blessed be thou among women and blessed be the fruit of thy womb!'"

Second Point. Second: Our Lady sings the canticle, saying: "`My soul doth magnify the Lord!'"

Third Point. Third: "Mary abode with Elizabeth about three months: and then she returned to her house."

OF THE BIRTH OF CHRIST OUR LORD

St. Luke speaks in the second Chapter [**1-15**].

First Point. First: Our Lady and her husband Joseph go from Nazareth to Bethlehem. "Joseph went up from Galilee to Bethlehem, to acknowledge subjection to Caesar, with Mary his spouse and wife, already with child."

Second Point. Second: "She brought forth her first-born Son and wrapped Him up with swaddling clothes and laid Him in the manger."

Third Point. Third: "There came a multitude of the heavenly army, which said: `Glory be to God in the heavens.'"

OF THE SHEPHERDS

St. Luke writes in the second Chapter [**8-21**].

First Point. First: The birth of Christ our Lord is manifested to the Shepherds by the Angel. "`I manifest to you great Joy, for this day is born the Saviour of the world."`

Second Point. Second: The Shepherds go to Bethlehem. "They came with haste and they found Mary and Joseph, and the infant put in the manger."

Third Point. Third: "The Shepherds returned glorifying and praising the Lord."

OF THE CIRCUMCISION

St. Luke writes in the second Chapter [**21**].

First Point. First: They circumcised the Child Jesus.

Second Point. Second: "His Name was called Jesus, which was called by the Angel, before He was conceived in the womb."

Third Point. Third: They gave back the Child to His Mother, who had compassion for the Blood which came from her Son.

OF THE THREE MAGI KINGS

St. Matthew writes in the second Chapter [**1-13**].

First Point. First: The three Magi Kings, guiding themselves by the star, came to adore Jesus, saying: "`We have seen His star in the East and are come to adore Him.'"

Second Point. Second: They adored Him and offered gifts to Him. "Falling down on the earth, they adored Him, and they offered Him gifts, gold, frankincense and myrrh."

Third Point. Third: "They received answer while sleeping that they should not return to Herod, and went back by another way to their country."

OF THE PURIFICATION OF OUR LADY AND PRESENTATION OF THE CHILD JESUS

St. Luke writes, Chapter **2** [**23-39**].

First Point. First: They bring the Child Jesus to the Temple, that He may be presented to the Lord as first-born; and they offer for Him "a pair of turtle doves or two young pigeons."

Second Point. Second: Simeon coming to the Temple "took Him into his arms" saying: "`Now Thou dost dismiss Thy servant, O Lord, in peace!'"

Third Point. Third: Anna "coming afterwards confessed to the Lord, and spoke of Him to all that were hoping for the redemption of Israel."

OF THE FLIGHT TO EGYPT

St. Matthew writes in the second Chapter [**13-16**].

First Point. First: Herod wanted to kill the Child Jesus, and so killed the Innocents, and before their death the Angel warned Joseph to fly into Egypt: "`Arise and take the Child and His Mother, and fly to Egypt.'"

Second Point. Second: He departed for Egypt. "Who arising by night departed to Egypt."

Third Point. Third: He was there until the death of Herod.

OF HOW CHRIST OUR LORD RETURNED FROM EGYPT

St. Matthew writes in the second Chapter [**19-23**].

First Point. First: The Angel warns Joseph to return to Israel. "`Arise and take the Child and His Mother and go to the land of Israel.'"

Second Point. Second: Rising, he came to the land of Israel.

Third Point. Third: Because Archelaus, son of Herod, was reigning in Judea, he withdrew into Nazareth.

OF THE LIFE OF CHRIST OUR LORD FROM TWELVE TO THIRTY YEARS

St. Luke writes in the second Chapter [**51, 52**].

First Point. First: He was obedient to His parents: “He advanced in wisdom, age and grace.”

Second Point. Second: It appears that [**24**] He exercised the trade of carpenter, as St. Mark shows he means[**25**] in the sixth chapter. “`Perhaps this is that carpenter? `”

OF THE COMING OF CHRIST TO THE TEMPLE WHEN HE WAS OF THE AGE OF TWELVE YEARS

St. Luke writes in the second Chapter [**42-51**].

First Point. First: Christ our Lord, of the age of twelve years, went up from Nazareth to Jerusalem.

Second Point. Second: Christ our Lord remained in Jerusalem, and His parents did not know it.

Third Point. Third: The three days passed, they found Him disputing in the Temple, and seated in the midst of the doctors, and His parents asking Him where He had been, He answered: “`Did you not know that it behooves Me to be in the things which are My Father's?'”

OF HOW CHRIST WAS BAPTIZED

St. Matthew writes in the third Chapter [**13-17**].

First Point. First: Christ our Lord, after having taken leave of His Blessed Mother, came from Nazareth to the River Jordan, where St. John Baptist was.

Second Point. Second: St. John baptized Christ our Lord, and wanting to excuse himself, thinking himself unworthy of baptizing Him, Christ said to him: “Do this for the present, for so it is necessary that we fulfill all justice.'”

Third Point. Third: “The Holy Spirit came and the voice of the Father from heaven affirming: `This is My beloved Son, in Whom I am well pleased.'"

OF HOW CHRIST WAS TEMPTED

St. Luke writes in the fourth Chapter [**1-14**] and St. Matthew fourth Chapter [**1-12**].

First Point. First: After being baptized, He went to the Desert, where He fasted forty days and forty nights.

Second Point. Second: He was tempted by the enemy three times. "The tempter coming to Him said to Him: `If Thou be the Son of God, say that these stones be turned into bread.' `Cast Thyself down from here.' `If prostrate on the earth Thou wilt adore me, I will give Thee all this which Thou seest.'"

Third Point. Third: "The Angels came and ministered to Him."

OF THE CALL OF THE APOSTLES

First Point. First: it seems that[**26**] St. Peter and St. Andrew were called three times: first, to some knowledge; this is clear from St. John in the first Chapter: secondly, to follow Christ in some way with the purpose of returning to possess what they had left, as St. Luke says in the fifth Chapter: thirdly, to follow Christ our Lord forever, as St. Matthew says in the fourth Chapter and St. Mark in the first.

Second Point. Second: He called Philip, as is in the first Chapter of St. John, and Matthew as Matthew himself says in the ninth Chapter.

Third Point. Third: He called the other Apostles, of whose special call the Gospel does not make mention.

And three other things also would be to be considered:

The first, how the Apostles were of uneducated and low condition;

The second, the dignity to which they were so sweetly called;

The third, the gifts and graces by which they were raised above all the Fathers of the New and Old Testaments.

OF THE FIRST MIRACLE PERFORMED AT THE MARRIAGE OF CANA, GALILEE

St. John writes Chapter **2** [**1-12**].

First Point. First: Christ our Lord was invited with His Disciples to the marriage.

Second Point. Second: The Mother tells her Son of the failure of the wine, saying: "`They have no wine,'"and bade the servants: "`Whatsoever He shall say to you, do ye.'"

Third Point. Third: "He changed the water into wine and manifested His glory, and His Disciples believed in Him."

OF HOW CHRIST CAST OUT OF THE TEMPLE THOSE WHO WERE SELLING

St. John writes Chapter **2** [**13-18**].

First Point. First: With a whip made of cords, He cast out of the Temple all those who were selling.

Second Point. Second: He turned over the tables and money of the rich bankers who were in the Temple.

Third Point. Third: To the poor who sold doves, He mildly said: "`Take these things from here, and make not My house a house of traffic.'"

OF THE SERMON WHICH CHRIST MADE ON THE MOUNT

St. Matthew writes in the fifth Chapter [**1-48**].

First Point. First: To His beloved Disciples He speaks apart about the Eight Beatitudes: "`Blessed the poor of spirit, the meek, the merciful, those who weep, those who suffer hunger and thirst for justice, the clean of heart, the peaceful, and those who suffer persecution.'"

Second Point. Second: He exhorts them to use their talents well: "`So let your light shine before men, that they may see your good works and glorify your Father Who is in the heavens.'"

Third Point. Third: He shows Himself not a transgressor, but a perfector of the law; explaining the precept of not killing, not committing fornication, not being guilty of perjury, and of loving enemies. "`I say to you that you love your enemies and do good to them that hate you.'"

OF HOW CHRIST OUR LORD MADE THE TEMPEST OF THE SEA BE CALM

St. Matthew writes Chapter **8** [**23-28**].

First Point. First: Christ our Lord being asleep at sea, a great tempest[**27**] arose.

Second Point. Second: His Disciples, frightened, awakened Him. Whom He reprehends for the little faith which they had, saying to them: "`What do you fear, ye of little faith!'"

Third Point. Third: He commanded the winds and the sea to cease: and, so ceasing, the sea became calm: at which the men wondered, saying: "`Who is this whom the wind and the sea obey?'"

OF HOW CHRIST WALKED ON THE SEA

St. Matthew writes Chapter **14** [**22-34**].

First Point. First: Christ our Lord being on the mountain, made His Disciples go to the little boat. And having dismissed the multitude, He commenced to pray alone.

Second Point. Second: The little boat was beaten by the waves. To which Christ came walking on the water; and the Disciples thought it was an apparition.

Third Point. Third: Christ saying to them: "`It is I, fear not,'" St. Peter, by His command, came to Him walking on the water. Doubting, he commenced to sink, but Christ our Lord freed him and reprehended him for his little faith, and then, as He entered into the little boat, the wind ceased.

OF HOW THE APOSTLES WERE SENT TO PREACH

St. Matthew writes in the tenth Chapter

First Point. First: Christ called His beloved Disciples and gave them power to cast out the demons from human bodies and to cure all the diseases.

Second Point. Second: He teaches them of prudence and patience: "`Behold, I send you as sheep in the midst of wolves. Be ye therefore wise as serpents and simple as doves.'"

Third Point. Third: He gives them the way to go. "`Do not want to possess gold nor silver: what you have freely received, freely give.'" And He gave them matter to preach. "`Going you shall preach, saying: `The Kingdom of Heaven has approached.'"

OF THE CONVERSION OF MAGDALEN

St. Luke writes in the seventh Chapter [**36-50**].

First Point. First: Magdalen enters where Christ our Lord is seated at the table in the house of the Pharisee. She bore a vase of alabaster full of ointment.

Second Point. Second: Standing behind the Lord near His feet, she commenced to wash them with tears and dried them with the hairs of her head, and kissed His feet and anointed them with ointment.

Third Point. Third: When the Pharisee accused Magdalen, Christ speaks in her defence, saying: "`Many sins are forgiven her because she loves much.' And He said to the woman: `Thy faith hath made thee safe: go in peace.'"

OF HOW CHRIST OUR LORD GAVE TO EAT FIVE THOUSAND MEN

St. Matthew writes in the fourteenth Chapter [**13-22**].

First Point. First: The Disciples, as it was getting late, ask Christ to dismiss the multitude of men who were with Him.

Second Point. Second: Christ our Lord commands that they bring Him bread, and commanded that they should be seated at the table, and blessed and broke and gave the bread to His Disciples, and the Disciples to the multitude.

Third Point. Third: "They did eat and were filled and there were twelve baskets over."

OF THE TRANSFIGURATION OF CHRIST

St. Matthew writes in the seventeenth Chapter [**1-14**].

First Point. First: Taking along His beloved Disciples, Peter, James, John, Christ our Lord was transfigured, and His face did shine as the sun, and His garments as the snow.

Second Point. Second: He was speaking with Moses and Elias.

Third Point. Third: St. Peter saying that they would make three tabernacles, a voice from heaven sounded, which said: "`This is My beloved Son, hear ye Him!'" When His Disciples heard this voice, they fell for fear on their faces; and

Christ our Lord touched them and said to them: "` Arise and fear not. Tell this vision to no one until the Son of Man be risen.'"

OF THE RESURRECTION OF LAZARUS

John, Chapter **11** [**1-46**].

First Point. First: Martha and Mary sent word to Christ our Lord of the illness of Lazarus. Knowing it, He delayed for two days, that the miracle might be more evident.

Second Point. Second: Before He raises him, He asks the one and the other to believe, saying: "`I am the resurrection and life; he who believeth in Me, although he be dead, shall live.'"

Third Point. Third: He raises him, after having wept and prayed. And the manner of raising him was by commanding: "`Lazarus, come forth!'"

OF THE SUPPER AT BETHANY

Matthew, Chapter **26** [**1-14**].

First Point. First: The Lord sups in the house of Simon the Leper, along with Lazarus.

Second Point. Second: Mary pours the ointment on the head of Christ.

Third Point. Third: Judas murmurs, saying: "`For what is this waste of ointment?'" But He a second time excuses Magdalen, saying: "`Why are you troublesome to this woman? for she hath wrought a good work upon Me.'"

PALM SUNDAY

Matthew, Chapter **21** [**1-12**].

First Point. First: The Lord sends for the ass and the foal, saying: "Loose them and bring them to Me, and if any one shall say anything to you, say ye that the Lord hath need of them, and forthwith he will let them go."

Second Point. Second: He mounted upon the ass, which was covered with the garments of the Apostles.

Third Point. Third: They went out to receive Him, strewing in the way their garments and the branches of the trees, saying: "`Save us, Son of David, blessed is He that cometh in the name of the Lord: Save us in the heights!'"

OF THE PREACHING IN THE TEMPLE

Luke, Chapter **19** [**47**, **48**].

First Point. First: He was every day teaching in the Temple.

Second Point. Second: The preaching finished, since there was no one who would receive Him in Jerusalem, He used to return to Bethany.

OF THE SUPPER

Matthew **26**; John **13**.

First Point. First: He ate the Paschal Lamb with His twelve Apostles, to whom He foretold His death. "`In truth, I say to you that one of you is to sell Me.'"

Second Point. Second: He washed the Disciples' feet, even those of Judas, commencing from St. Peter, who, considering the Majesty of the Lord and his own baseness, not wanting to consent, said: "Lord, dost Thou wash my feet?" But St. Peter did not know that in that He gave an example of humility, and for this He said: "`I have given you an example, that you may do as I did.'"

Third Point. Third: He instituted the most sacred sacrifice of the Eucharist, to be the greatest mark of His love, saying: "`Take and eat.'" The Supper finished, Judas went forth to sell Christ our Lord.

OF THE MYSTERIES DONE FROM THE SUPPER TO THE GARDEN, INCLUSIVE

Matthew, Chapter **26**, and Mark, Chapter **14**.

First Point. First: The Supper finished, and singing the hymn, the Lord went to Mount Olivet with His Disciples, who were full of fear; and leaving the eight in Gethsemani, He said: "`Sit ye here till I go yonder to pray.'"

Second Point. Second: Accompanied by St. Peter, St. James and St. John, He prayed three times to the Lord, saying: "`Father, if it be possible, let this chalice pass from Me. Nevertheless, let not My will be done, but Thine.'" And being in agony, He prayed the longer.

Third Point. Third: He came into such fear, that He said: "`My soul is sorrowful unto death,'" and He sweated blood so plentiful, that St. Luke says: "His sweat was as drops of blood which were running on the earth;" which supposes that the garments were already full of blood.

OF THE MYSTERIES DONE FROM THE GARDEN TO THE HOUSE OF ANNAS, INCLUSIVE

Matthew **26**, Luke **22**, Mark **15**.

First Point. First: The Lord lets Himself be kissed by Judas and taken as a robber, to whom He said: "`You have come out as to a robber to apprehend Me with clubs and arms; when I was daily with you in the Temple teaching and you did not take Me."` And He saying: "`Whom seek ye?"` the enemies fell on the earth.

Second Point. Second: St. Peter wounded a servant of the High Priest, and the meek Lord said to Peter: "`Return thy sword into its place,'" and He healed the wound of the servant.

Third Point. Third: Left by His Disciples, He is taken to Annas, where St. Peter, who had followed Him from afar, denied Him once, and a blow was given Christ by one saying to Him: "`Answerest Thou the High Priest so?"`

OF THE MYSTERIES DONE FROM THE HOUSE OF ANNAS TO THE HOUSE OF CAIPHAS, INCLUSIVE

First Point. First: They take Him bound from the house of Annas to the house of Caiphas, where St. Peter denied Him twice, and looked at by the Lord, going forth he wept bitterly.

Second Point. Second: Jesus was all that night bound.

Third Point. Third: Besides, those who held Him captive mocked Him and struck Him and covered His face and gave Him buffets and asked Him: "`Prophesy to us, who is he that struck Thee?'" and like things, blaspheming against Him.

OF THE MYSTERIES DONE FROM THE HOUSE OF CAIPHAS TO THAT OF PILATE, INCLUSIVE

Matthew **26**, Luke **23**, Mark **15**.

First Point. First: The whole multitude of the Jews **[28]** take Him to Pilate and accuse Him before him, saying: "`We have found that this man tried to ruin our people and forbade to pay tribute to Caesar.'"

Second Point. Second: Pilate, after having examined Him once and again, said: "`I find no fault.'"

Third Point. Third: The robber Barabbas was preferred to Him. "They all cried, saying: `Give us not this man, but Barabbas!'"

OF THE MYSTERIES DONE FROM THE HOUSE OF PILATE TO THAT OF HEROD

First Point. First: Pilate sent Jesus, a Galilean, to Herod, Tetrarch of Galilee.

Second Point. Second: Herod, curious, questioned Him much and He answered him nothing, although the Scribes and Priests were accusing Him constantly.

Third Point. Third: Herod despised Him with his army, clothing Him with a white garment.

OF THE MYSTERIES DONE FROM THE HOUSE OF HEROD TO THAT OF PILATE

Matthew **26**,[**29**] Luke **23**, Mark **15**, and John **19**.

First Point. First: Herod sends Him back to Pilate. By this they were made friends, who before were enemies.

Second Point. Second: Pilate took Jesus and scourged Him; and the soldiers made a crown of thorns and put it on His head, and they clothed Him with purple and came to Him and said: "`Hail, King of the Jews!'", and they gave Him buffets.

Third Point. Third: He brought Him forth in the presence of all. "Then Jesus went forth crowned with thorns and clothed with a purple garment, and Pilate said to them: `Here is the Man!'" and when the Priests saw Him, they shouted, saying: "`Crucify, crucify Him!'"

OF THE MYSTERIES DONE FROM THE HOUSE OF PILATE TO THE CROSS, INCLUSIVE

John **19** [**15-20**].

First Point. First: Pilate, seated as judge, delivered Jesus to them to crucify Him, after the Jews had denied Him for king, saying: "`We have no king but Caesar!`"

Second Point. Second: He took the Cross on His shoulders and not being able to carry it, Simon of Cyrene was constrained to carry it after Jesus.

Third Point. Third: They crucified Him between two thieves, setting this title: "Jesus of Nazareth, King of the Jews."

OF THE MYSTERIES ON THE CROSS

John **19** [**25-37**].

First Point. First: He spoke seven words on the Cross: He prayed for those who were crucifying Him; He pardoned the thief; He recommended St. John to His Mother and His Mother to St. John; He said with a loud voice: "`I thirst,'" and they gave Him gall and vinegar; He said that He was abandoned; He said: "It is consummated"; He said: "Father, into Thy hands I commend My spirit!"

Second Point. Second: The sun was darkened, the stones broken, the graves opened, the veil of the Temple was rent in two from above below.[**30**]

Third Point. Third: They blaspheme Him, saying: "`Thou wert He who destroyest the Temple of God; come down from the Cross."` His garments were divided; His side, struck with the lance, sent forth water and blood.

OF THE MYSTERIES FROM THE CROSS TO THE SEPULCHRE, INCLUSIVE

Ibidem.

First Point. First: He was let down from the Cross by Joseph and Nicodemus, in presence of His sorrowful Mother.

Second Point. Second: The Body was carried to the Sepulchre and anointed and buried.

Third Point. Third: Guards were set.

OF THE RESURRECTION OF CHRIST OUR LORD OF HIS FIRST APPARITION

First Point. First: He appeared to the Virgin Mary. This, although it is not said in Scripture, is included in saying that He appeared to so many others, because Scripture supposes that we have understanding,[**31**] as it is written: "`Are you also without understanding?"`

OF THE SECOND APPARITION

Mark, Chapter **16** [**9**].

First Point. First: Mary Magdalen, Mary, the mother of James, and Salome come very[**32**] early to the Sepulchre saying: "`Who shall lift for us the stone from the door of the Sepulchre?'"

Second Point. Second: They see the stone lifted, and the Angel, who says: "`You seek Jesus of Nazareth. He is already risen, He is not here.'"

Third Point. Third: He appeared to Mary, who remained about the Sepulchre after the others had gone.

OF THE THIRD APPARITION

St. Matthew, last Chapter.

First Point. First: These Maries go from the Sepulchre with fear and joy, wanting to announce to the Disciples the Resurrection of the Lord.

Second Point. Second: Christ our Lord appeared to them on the way, saying to them: "Hail:" and they approached and threw themselves at His feet and adored Him.

Third Point. Third: Jesus says to them: "`Fear not! Go and tell My brethren that they go into Galilee, for there they shall see Me.'"

OF THE FOURTH APPARITION

Last Chapter of Luke [**12, 34**].

First Point. First: Having heard from the women that Christ was risen, St. Peter went quickly to the Sepulchre.

Second Point. Second: Entering into the Sepulchre, he saw only the cloths with which the Body of Christ our Lord had been covered, and nothing else.

Third Point. Third: As St. Peter was thinking of these things, Christ appeared to Him, and therefore the Apostles said: "`Truly the Lord has risen and appeared to Simon.'"

OF THE FIFTH APPARITION

In the last Chapter of St. Luke.

First Point. First: He appeared to the Disciples who were going to Emmaus, talking of Christ.

Second Point. Second: He reproves them, showing by the Scriptures that Christ had to die and rise again: "`O foolish and slow of heart to believe all that the Prophets have spoken! Was it not necessary that Christ should suffer and so enter into His glory?"`

Third Point. Third: At their prayer, He lingers there, and was with them until, in giving them Communion, He disappeared. And they, returning, told the Disciples how they had known Him in the Communion.

OF THE SIXTH APPARITION

John, Chapter **20** [**19-24**].

First Point. First: The Disciples, except St. Thomas, were gathered together for fear of the Jews.

Second Point. Second: Jesus appeared to them, the doors being shut, and being in the midst of them, He says: "`Peace be with you!'"

Third Point. Third: He gives them the Holy Ghost, saying to them: "`Receive ye the Holy Ghost: to those whose sins you shall forgive, to them they shall be forgiven.'"

THE SEVENTH APPARITION

John **20** [**24-30**].

First Point. First: St. Thomas, incredulous because he was absent from the preceding apparition, says: "If I do not see Him, I will not believe."

Second Point. Second: Jesus appears to them eight days from that, the doors being shut, and says to St. Thomas: "`Put here thy finger and see the truth; and be not incredulous, but believing.'"

Third Point. Third: St. Thomas believed, saying: "`My Lord and my God!" Christ said to him: "`Blessed are those who have not seen and have believed.'"

OF THE EIGHTH APPARITION

John, last Chapter [**1-24**].

First Point. First: Jesus appears to seven of His Disciples[**33**] who were fishing, and had taken nothing all night; and spreading the net by His command, "They were not able to draw it out for the multitude of the fishes."

Second Point. Second: By this miracle St. John knew Him and said to St. Peter: "`It is the Lord!'" He cast himself into the sea and came to Christ.

Third Point. Third: He gave them to eat part of a fish roasted, and a comb of honey,[**34**] and recommended the sheep to St. Peter, having first examined him three times on charity, and says to him: "`Feed My sheep! `"

OF THE NINTH APPARITION

Matthew, last Chapter [**16**-end].

First Point. First: The Disciples, by command of the Lord, go to Me. Thabor.

Second Point. Second: Christ appears to them and says: "`All power is given to Me in heaven and on earth.'"

Third Point. Third: He sent them through all the world to preach, saying: "`Go and teach ye all nations, baptizing them in the name of the Father and of the Son and of the Holy Ghost.'"

OF THE TENTH APPARITION

In the First Epistle to the Corinthians, Chapter **15** [**7**]. "Afterwards He was seen by more than five hundred brethren together."

OF THE ELEVENTH APPARITION

In the First Epistle to the Corinthians, Chapter **15** [**7**]. "Afterwards He appeared to St. James."

OF THE TWELFTH APPARITION

He appeared to Joseph of Arimathea, as is piously meditated and is read in the lives of the Saints.[**35**]

OF THE THIRTEENTH APPARITION

First Epistle to the Corinthians, Chapter **15** [**8**]. He appeared to St. Paul after the Ascension. "`Last of all, He appeared to me, as one born out of due time.'"

He appeared also in soul to the Holy Fathers of Limbo, and after taking them out and having taken His Body again, He appeared to the Disciples many times, and dealt with them.

OF THE ASCENSION OF CHRIST OUR LORD

Acts **1** [**1-12**].

First Point. First: After He appeared for the space of forty days to the Apostles, giving many arguments and doing many signs, and speaking of the kingdom of God, He bade them await in Jerusalem the Holy Ghost promised.

Second Point. Second: He brought them out to Mt. Olivet, and in their presence He was raised up and a cloud made Him disappear from their eyes.

Third Point. Third: They looking to heaven, the Angels say to them: "`Men of Galilee, why stand you looking to heaven? This Jesus, Who is taken from your eyes to heaven, shall so come as you saw Him go into heaven.'"

XIII. Rules

RULES FOR PERCEIVING AND KNOWING IN SOME MANNER THE DIFFERENT MOVEMENTS WHICH ARE CAUSED IN THE SOUL

The Good, To Receive Them, And The Bad To Reject Them. And They Are More Proper For The First Week.

First Rule. The first Rule: In the persons who go from mortal sin to mortal sin, the enemy is commonly used to propose to them apparent pleasures, making them imagine sensual delights and pleasures in order to hold them more and make them grow in their vices and sins. In these persons the good spirit uses the opposite method, pricking them and biting their consciences through the process of reason.

Second Rule. The second: In the persons who are going on intensely cleansing their sins and rising from good to better in the service of God our Lord, it is the method contrary to that in the first Rule, for then it is the way of the evil spirit to bite, sadden and put obstacles, disquieting with false reasons, that one may not go on; and it is proper to the good to give courage and strength, consolations, tears, inspirations and quiet, easing, and putting away all obstacles, that one may go on in well doing.

Third Rule. The third: OF SPIRITUAL CONSOLATION. I call it consolation when some interior movement in the soul is caused, through which the soul comes to be inflamed with love of its Creator and Lord; and when it can in consequence love no created thing on the face of the earth in itself, but in the Creator of them all.

Likewise, when it sheds tears that move to love of its Lord, whether out of sorrow for one's sins, or for the Passion of Christ our Lord, or because of other things directly connected with His service and praise.

Finally, I call consolation every increase of hope, faith and charity, and all interior joy which calls and attracts to heavenly things and to the salvation of one's soul, quieting it and giving it peace in its Creator and Lord.

Fourth Rule. The fourth: OF SPIRITUAL DESOLATION. I call desolation all the contrary of the third[**36**] rule, such as darkness[**37**] of soul, disturbance in it, movement to things low and earthly, the unquiet of different agitations and temptations, moving to want of confidence, without hope, without love, when one finds oneself all lazy, tepid, sad, and as if separated from his Creator and Lord. Because, as consolation is contrary to desolation, in the same way the thoughts which come from consolation are contrary to the thoughts which come from desolation.

Fifth Rule. The fifth: In time of desolation never to make a change; but to be firm and constant in the resolutions and determination in which one was the day preceding such desolation, or in the determination in which he was in the preceding consolation. Because, as in consolation it is rather the good spirit who guides and counsels us, so in desolation it is the bad, with whose counsels we cannot take a course to decide rightly.

Sixth Rule. The sixth: Although in desolation we ought not to change our first resolutions, it is very helpful intensely to change ourselves against the same desolation, as by insisting more on prayer, meditation, on much examination, and by giving ourselves more scope in some suitable way of doing penance.

Seventh Rule. The seventh: Let him who is in desolation consider how the Lord has left him in trial in his natural powers, in order to resist the different agitations and temptations of the enemy; since he can with the Divine help, which always remains to him, though he does not clearly perceive it: because the Lord has taken from him his great fervor, great love and intense grace, leaving him, however, grace enough for eternal salvation.

Eighth Rule. The eighth: Let him who is in desolation labor to be in patience, which is contrary to the vexations which come to him: and let him think that he will soon be consoled, employing against the desolation the devices, as is said in the sixth Rule. [**38**]

Ninth Rule. The ninth: There are three principal reasons why we find ourselves desolate.

The first is, because of our being tepid, lazy or negligent in our spiritual exercises; and so through our faults, spiritual consolation withdraws from us.

The second, to try us and see how much we are and how much we let ourselves out in His service and praise without such great pay of consolation and great graces.

The third, to give us true acquaintance and knowledge, that we may interiorly feel that it is not ours to get or keep great devotion, intense love, tears, or any other spiritual consolation, but that all is the gift and grace of God our Lord, and that we may not build a nest in a thing not ours, raising our intellect into some pride or vainglory, attributing to us devotion or the other things of the spiritual consolation.

Tenth Rule. The tenth: Let him who is in consolation think how he will be in the desolation which will come after, taking new strength for then.

Eleventh Rule. The eleventh: Let him who is consoled see to humbling himself and lowering himself as much as he can, thinking how little he is able for in the time of desolation without such grace or consolation.

On the contrary, let him who is in desolation think that he can do much with the grace sufficient to resist all his enemies, taking strength in his Creator and Lord.

Twelfth Rule. The twelfth: The enemy acts like a woman, in being weak against vigor and strong of will. Because, as it is the way of the woman when she is quarrelling with some man to lose heart, taking flight when the man shows her much courage: and on the contrary, if the man, losing heart, begins to fly, the wrath, revenge, and ferocity of the woman is very great, and so without bounds; in the same manner, it is the way of the enemy to weaken and lose heart, his temptations taking flight, when the person who is exercising himself in spiritual things opposes a bold front against the temptations of the enemy, doing diametrically the opposite. And on the contrary, if the person who is exercising himself commences to have fear and lose heart in suffering the temptations, there is no beast so wild on the face of the earth as the enemy of human nature in following out his damnable intention with so great malice.

Thirteenth Rule. The thirteenth: Likewise, he acts as a licentious lover in wanting to be secret and not revealed. For, as the licentious man who, speaking for an evil purpose, solicits a daughter of a good father or a wife of a good husband, wants his words and persuasions to be secret, and the contrary displeases him much, when the daughter reveals to her father or the wife to her husband his licentious words and depraved intention, because he easily gathers that he will not be able to succeed with the undertaking begun: in the same way, when the enemy of human nature brings his wiles and persuasions to the just soul, he wants and desires that they be received and kept in secret; but when one reveals them to his good Confessor or to another spiritual person that knows his deceits and evil ends, it is very grievous to him, because he gathers, from his manifest deceits being discovered, that he will not be able to succeed with his wickedness begun.

Fourteenth Rule. The fourteenth: Likewise, he behaves as a chief bent on conquering and robbing what he desires: for, as a captain and chief of the army, pitching his camp, and looking at the forces or defences of a stronghold, attacks it on the weakest side, in like manner the enemy of human nature, roaming about, looks in turn at all our virtues, theological, cardinal and moral; and where he finds us weakest and most in need for our eternal salvation, there he attacks us and aims at taking us.

RULES FOR THE SAME EFFECT WITH GREATER DISCERNMENT OF SPIRITS AND THEY HELP MORE FOR THE SECOND WEEK

First Rule. The first: It is proper to God and to His Angels in their movements to give true spiritual gladness and joy, taking away all sadness and disturbance which the enemy brings on. Of this latter it is proper to fight against the spiritual gladness and consolation, bringing apparent reasons, subtleties and continual fallacies.

Second Rule. The second: It belongs to God our Lord to give consolation to the soul without preceding cause, for it is the property of the Creator to enter, go out and cause movements in the soul, bringing it all into love of His Divine Majesty. I say without cause: without any previous sense or knowledge of any object through which such consolation would come, through one's acts of understanding and will.

Third Rule. The third: With cause, as well the good Angel as the bad can console the soul, for contrary ends: the good Angel for the profit of the soul, that it may grow and rise from good to better, and the evil Angel, for the contrary, and later on to draw it to his damnable intention and wickedness.

Fourth Rule. The fourth: It is proper to the evil Angel, who forms himself under the appearance of an angel of light, to enter with the devout soul and go out with himself: that is to say, to bring good and holy thoughts, conformable to such just soul, and then little by little he aims at coming out drawing the soul to his covert deceits and perverse intentions.

Fifth Rule. The fifth: We ought to note well the course of the thoughts, and if the beginning, middle and end is all good, inclined to all good, it is a sign of the good Angel; but if in the course of the thoughts which he brings it ends in something bad, of a distracting tendency, or less good than what the soul had previously proposed to do, or if it weakens it or disquiets or disturbs the soul, taking away its peace, tranquillity and quiet, which it had before, it is a clear sign that it proceeds from the evil spirit, enemy of our profit and eternal salvation.

Sixth Rule. The sixth: When the enemy of human nature has been perceived and known by his serpent's tail and the bad end to which he leads on, it helps the person who was tempted by him, to look immediately at the course of the good thoughts which he brought him at their beginning, and how little by little he aimed at making him descend from the spiritual sweetness and joy in which he was, so far as to bring him to his depraved intention; in order that with this experience, known and noted, the person may be able to guard for the future against his usual deceits.

Seventh Rule. The seventh: In those who go on from good to better, the good Angel touches such soul sweetly, lightly and gently, like a drop of water which enters into a sponge; and the evil touches it sharply and with noise and disquiet, as when the drop of water falls on the stone.

And the above-said spirits touch in a contrary way those who go on from bad to worse.

The reason of this is that the disposition of the soul is contrary or like to the said Angels. Because, when it is contrary, they enter perceptibly with clatter and noise; and when it is like, they enter with silence as into their own home, through the open door.

Eighth Rule. The eighth: When the consolation is without cause, although there be no deceit in it, as being of God our Lord alone, as was said; still the spiritual person to whom God gives such consolation, ought, with much vigilance and attention, to look at and distinguish the time itself of such actual consolation from the following, in which the soul remains warm and favored with the favor and remnants of the consolation past; for often in this second time, through one's own course of habits and the consequences of the concepts and judgments, or through the good spirit or through the bad, he forms various resolutions and opinions which are not given immediately by God our Lord, and therefore they have need to be very well examined before entire credit is given them, or they are put into effect.

IN THE MINISTRY OF DISTRIBUTING ALMS THE FOLLOWING RULES SHOULD BE KEPT

First Rule. The first: If I make the distribution to relatives or friends, or to persons for whom I have an affection, I shall have four things to see to, of which mention was made, in part, in the matter of Election.

The first is, that that love which moves me and makes me give the alms, should descend from above, from the love of God our Lord, so that I feel first in me that the love, more or less, which I have to such persons is for God; and that in the reason why I love them more, God appears.

Second Rule. The second: I want to set before me a man whom I have never seen or known, and desiring all his perfection in the ministry and condition which he has, as I would want him to keep the mean in his manner of distributing, for the greater glory of God our Lord and the greater perfection of his soul; I, doing so, neither more nor less, will keep the rule and measure which I should want and judge to be right for the other.

Third Rule. The third: I want to consider, as if I were at the point of death, the form and measure which then I should want to have kept in the office of my administration, and regulating myself by that, to keep it in the acts of my distribution.

Fourth Rule. The fourth: Looking how I shall find myself on the Day of Judgment, to think well how then I should want to have used this office and charge of administration; and the rule which then I should want to have kept, to keep it now.

Fifth Rule. The fifth: When some person feels himself inclined and drawn to some persons to whom he wants to distribute alms, let him hold himself back and ponder well the above-mentioned four Rules, examining and testing his affection by them; and not give the alms until, conformably to them, he has in all dismissed and cast out his disordered inclination.

Sixth Rule. The sixth: Although there is no fault in taking the goods of God our Lord to distribute them, when the person is called by God our Lord to such ministry; still in the quantity of what he has to take and apply to himself out of what he has to give to others, there may be doubt as to fault and excess. Therefore, he can reform in his life and condition by the above-mentioned Rules.

Seventh Rule. The seventh: For the reasons already mentioned and for many others, it is always better and more secure in what touches one's person and condition of life to spare more and diminish and approach more to our High Priest, our model and rule, who is Christ our Lord; conformably to what the third Council of Carthage, in which St. Augustine was, determines and orders – that the furniture of the Bishop be cheap and poor. The same should be considered in all manners of life, looking at and deciding according to the condition and state of the persons; as in married life we have the example of St. Joachim and of St. Ann, who, dividing their means into three parts, gave the first to the poor, and the second to the ministry and service of the Temple, and took the third for the support of themselves and of their household.

THE FOLLOWING NOTES HELP TO PERCEIVE AND UNDERSTAND SCRUPLES AND PERSUASIONS OF OUR ENEMY

First Note. The first: They commonly call a scruple what proceeds from our own judgment and freedom: that is to say, when I freely decide that that is sin which is not sin, as when it happens that after some one has accidentally stepped on a cross of straw, he decides with his own judgment that he has sinned.

This is properly an erroneous judgment and not a real scruple.

Second Note. The second: After I have stepped on that cross, or after I have thought or said or done some other thing, there comes to me a thought from without that I have sinned, and on the other hand it appears to me that I have not sinned; still I feel disturbance in this; that is to say, in as much as I doubt and in as much as I do not doubt.

That is a real scruple and temptation which the enemy sets.

Third Note. Third: The first scruple – of the first note – is much to be abhorred, because it is all error; but the second – of the second note – for some space of time is of no little profit to the soul which is giving itself to spiritual exercises;[**39**] rather in great manner it purifies and cleanses such a soul, separating it much from all appearance of sin: according to that saying of Gregory: "It belongs to good minds to see a fault where there is no fault."

Fourth Note. The fourth: The enemy looks much if a soul is gross or delicate, and if it is delicate, he tries to make it more delicate in the extreme, to disturb and embarrass it more. For instance, if he sees that a soul does not consent to either mortal sin or venial or any appearance of deliberate sin, then the enemy, when he cannot make it fall into a thing that appears sin, aims at making it make out sin where there is not sin, as in a word or very small thought.

If the soul is gross, the enemy tries to make it more gross; for instance, if before it made no account of venial sins, he will try to have it make little account of mortal sins, and if before it made some account, he will try to have it now make much less or none.

Fifth Note. The fifth: The soul which desires to benefit itself in the spiritual life, ought always to proceed the contrary way to what the enemy proceeds; that is to say, if the enemy wants to make the soul gross, let it aim at making itself delicate. Likewise, if the enemy tries to draw it out to extreme fineness, let the soul try to establish itself in the mean, in order to quiet itself in everything.

Sixth Note. The sixth: When such good soul wants to speak or do something within the Church, within the understanding of our Superiors, and which should be for the glory of God our Lord, and there comes to him a thought or temptation from without that he should neither say nor do that thing – bringing to him apparent reasons of vainglory or of another thing, etc., – then he ought to raise his understanding to his Creator and Lord, and if he sees that it is His due service, or at the least not contrary to it, he ought to act diametrically against such temptation, according to St. Bernard, answering the same: "Neither for thee did I begin, nor for thee will I stop."

TO HAVE THE TRUE SENTIMENT WHICH WE OUGHT TO HAVE IN THE CHURCH MILITANT

Let the following Rules be observed.

First Rule. The first: All judgment laid aside, we ought to have our mind ready and prompt to obey, in all, the true Spouse of Christ our Lord, which is our holy Mother the Church Hierarchical.

Second Rule. The second: To praise confession to a Priest, and the reception of the most Holy Sacrament of the Altar once in the year, and much more each month, and much better from week to week, with the conditions required and due.

Third Rule. The third: To praise the hearing of Mass often, likewise[**40**] hymns, psalms, and long prayers, in the church and out of it; likewise the hours set at the time fixed for each Divine Office and for all prayer and all Canonical Hours.

Fourth Rule. The fourth: To praise much Religious Orders, virginity and continence, and not so much marriage as any of these.

Fifth Rule. The fifth: To praise vows of Religion, of obedience, of poverty, of chastity and of other perfections of supererogation. And it is to be noted that as the vow is about the things which approach to Evangelical perfection, a vow ought not to be made in the things which withdraw from it, such as to be a merchant, or to be married, etc.

Sixth Rule. To praise relics of the Saints, giving veneration to them and praying to the Saints; and to praise Stations, pilgrimages, Indulgences, pardons, Cruzadas, and candles lighted in the churches.

Seventh Rule. To praise Constitutions about fasts and abstinence, as of Lent, Ember Days, Vigils, Friday and Saturday; likewise penances, not only interior, but also exterior.

Eighth Rule. To praise the ornaments and the buildings of churches; likewise images, and to venerate them according to what they represent.

Ninth Rule. Finally, to praise all precepts of the Church, keeping the mind prompt to find reasons in their defence and in no manner against them.

Tenth Rule. We ought to be more prompt to find good and praise as well the Constitutions and recommendations as the ways of our Superiors. Because, although some are not or have not been such, to speak against them, whether preaching in public or discoursing before the common people, would rather give rise to fault-finding and scandal than profit; and so the people would be incensed against their Superiors, whether temporal or spiritual. So that, as it does harm to speak evil to the common people of Superiors in their absence, so it can make profit to speak of the evil ways to the persons themselves who can remedy them.

Eleventh Rule. To praise positive and scholastic learning. Because, as it is more proper to the Positive Doctors, as St. Jerome, St. Augustine and St. Gregory, etc., to move the heart to love and serve God our Lord in everything; so it is more proper to the Scholastics, as St. Thomas, St. Bonaventure, and to the Master of the Sentences, etc., to define or explain for our times [**41**] the things necessary for eternal salvation; and to combat and explain better all errors and all fallacies. For the Scholastic Doctors, as they are more modern, not only help themselves with the true understanding of the Sacred Scripture and of the Positive and holy Doctors, but also, they being enlightened and clarified by the Divine virtue, help themselves by the Councils, Canons and Constitutions of our holy Mother the Church.

Twelfth Rule. We ought to be on our guard in making comparison of those of us who are alive to the blessed passed away, because error is committed not a little in this; that is to say, in saying, this one knows more than St. Augustine; he is another, or greater than, St. Francis; he is another St. Paul in goodness, holiness, etc.

Thirteenth Rule. To be right in everything, we ought always to hold that the white which I see, is black, if the Hierarchical Church so decides it, believing that between Christ our Lord, the Bridegroom, and the Church, His Bride, there is the same Spirit which governs and directs us for the salvation of our souls. Because by the same Spirit and our Lord Who gave the ten Commandments, our holy Mother the Church is directed and governed.

Fourteenth Rule. Although there is much truth in the assertion that no one can save himself without being predestined and without having faith and grace; we must be very cautious in the manner of speaking and communicating with others about all these things.

Fifteenth Rule. We ought not, by way of custom, to speak much of predestination; but if in some way and at some times one speaks, let him so speak that the common people may not come into any error, as sometimes happens, saying: Whether I have to be saved or condemned is already determined, and no other thing can now be, through my doing well or ill; and with this, growing lazy, they become negligent in the works which lead to the salvation and the spiritual[**42**] profit of their souls.

Sixteenth Rule. In the same way, we must be on our guard that by talking much and with much insistence of faith, without any distinction and explanation, occasion be not given to the people to be lazy and slothful in works, whether before faith is formed in charity or after.

Seventeenth Rule. Likewise, we ought not to speak so much with insistence on grace that the poison of discarding liberty be engendered.

So that of faith and grace one can speak as much as is possible with the Divine help for the greater praise of His Divine Majesty, but not in such way, nor in such manners, especially in our so dangerous times, that works and free will receive any harm, or be held for nothing.

Eighteenth Rule. Although serving God our Lord much out of pure love is to be esteemed above all; we ought to praise much the fear of His Divine Majesty, because not only filial fear is a thing pious and most holy, but even servile fear – when the man reaches nothing else better or more useful – helps much to get out of mortal sin. And when he is out, he easily comes to filial fear, which is all acceptable and grateful to God our Lord: as being at one with the Divine Love.

THE END

Footnotes

[1] The word Annotation does not occur in the original after the first time. The same is true of similar cases in the Mss.

[2] Offering is in St. Ignatius' handwriting, correcting giving or presenting, which is crossed out.

[3] May make use of . . . according is in the Saint's handwriting, correcting some word erased.

[4] Without determining oneself through is in the Saint's hand, the words being inserted between life and tendency, the word without being cancelled.

[5] Synagogues is in the Saint's hand, replacing Temples, which is crossed out.

[6] It is doubtful whether these words are like me or with me.

[7] In Their Eternity is in St. Ignatius' hand, replacing among Them, which is cancelled.

[8] And so, the fullness of times being come is in the Saint's hand, and being crossed out.

[9] As can be piously meditated is in St. Ignatius' handwriting and is inserted before seated.

[10] The place or cave of the Nativity is in the Saint's hand, correcting the inn, which is crossed out.

[**11**] Great is inserted, perhaps in. the hand of St. Ignatius.

[**12**] As he is accustomed to do in most cases is inserted in the Saint's handwriting.

[**13**] Not solely or as they ought is a correction of not only, which is crossed out. The correction is perhaps in the handwriting of St. Ignatius.

[**14**] In the is in the Saint's hand, over a word erased.

[**15**] It does not appear that this election is a Divine vocation is in the Saint's hand, correcting we can not say that this election is His vocation.

[**16**] Divine is added in St. Ignatius' hand.

[**17**] I is added, perhaps in St. Ignatius' hand.

[**18**] To have is apparently in St. Ignatius' hand.

[**19**] In His Humanity is in St. Ignatius' hand, correcting the Humanity of before Christ.

[**20**] As drops of blood is in St. Ignatius' hand, replacing like a bloody sweat.

[**21**] Giving them to understand is an addition, very probably in St. Ignatius' hand.

[**22**] Making me to understand; likewise is in the Saint's handwriting, correcting a word erased, probably understanding.

[**23**] For the parentheses of the Mss. quotation marks have been substituted.

[**24**] It appears that is in the Saint's handwriting, inserted before He exercised.

[**25**] Shows he means is in the Saint's hand, correcting says.

[**26**] It seems that is added in the hand of St. Ignatius.

[**27**] Great tempest is in St. Ignatius' hand, correcting some word erased.

[**28**] The whole multitude of the Jews is inserted here in the handwriting of St. Ignatius, a phrase being erased after accuse.

[**29**] This should be **27**.

[**30**] Rent in two from above below is in St. Ignatius' handwriting, correcting torn in pieces, which is crossed out.

[**31**] Understanding is added, apparently in St. Ignatius' hand.

[**32**] Very is added, perhaps in St. Ignatius' hand.

[**33**] Of His Disciples is in the handwriting of St. Ignatius: replacing a word erased.

[**34**] These words are in St. Luke **24**, **42**.

[**35**] Is piously meditated and is read in the lives of the Saints is in the hand of St. Ignatius, replacing words which were apparently says the Gospel of Judea.

[**36**] Third is in the Saint's hand, replacing first.

[**37**] Darkness is perhaps in the Saint's handwriting, replacing blindness.

[**38**] Sixth Rule is in the handwriting of St. Ignatius, replacing fourth Rule.

[**39**] Exercises is added by St. Ignatius.

[**40**] Likewise is added in St. Ignatius' hand.

[**41**] Or explain for our times is added in the Saint's handwriting

[**42**] Spiritual is added in St. Ignatius' handwriting.

9 789373 680194

Printed at Repro India Ltd.